# NAPOLEON
# AND THE BATTLE OF WATERLOO

# NAPOLEON

## AND THE BATTLE OF

# WATERLOO

BY FRANCES WINWAR

*Illustrated by* DAVID STONE

RANDOM HOUSE · NEW YORK

FOURTH PRINTING

Copyright 1953 by Frances Winwar

All rights reserved under International and
Pan-American Copyright Conventions
Published in New York by Random House, Inc.
and simultaneously in Toronto, Canada by
Random House of Canada Ltd.
Library of Congress Catalog Card Number: 53-6272

Manufactured in the U.S.A.

*To*

JO-ANN AND DICKIE

*with love*

# CONTENTS

# NAPOLEON
# AND THE BATTLE OF WATERLOO

# [ 1 ]

## *The Corsican Boy*

THE YEAR 1769 WAS A RATHER PEACEFUL ONE
for Europe. There was trouble in Corsica, however. That rocky island in the Mediterranean, the
home of a rough, freedom-loving people, was in
revolt.

At one time Corsica had belonged to Genoa. But
the Corsicans wanted their country for themselves.
They gave Genoa so much trouble that the Genoese were forced to call on the French for aid against
the rebels. In return the French took possession of
the island.

The Corsicans did not like their new master any
better than the old, especially after the French

king sent an army to subdue them. Their spirit of independence was so aroused by this act that even the Corsican women joined their men in the fight.

Day and night the mountains echoed to the noise of battle. But the badly armed Corsicans were losing ground. When the French landed more forces the people took to the mountain hide-outs. They were so few and the French were so many!

To one of these rocky shelters one cold spring morning came Charles Buonaparte, a young lieutenant of the rebel leader, bringing food to his wife. Letizia Buonaparte looked so girlish, it was hard to believe that she was the mother of the fat little boy in her arms.

Charles Buonaparte laid a gourd of goat's milk and an oatmeal cake on a flat stone beside her.

"This is all I could find, Letizia," he said, stroking her hair. "How do you feel?"

She lifted up her face and smiled. "Well and happy when you are with me," she replied.

"Promise me you won't run out any more when

4

you hear the bullets whistling," he said. "You've got to think of our boy, you know, and of our next little son."

"Are you so sure it will be another boy?" She laughed.

"It must be a boy. Corsica needs men to fight for her."

Her eyes lighted up with pride. "Corsica will have another son," she said. "Pray God."

That son was born on the 15th of August, 1769, in the city of Ajaccio, shortly after Corsica fell to the French. His parents called him Napoleon. Unlike his brother Joseph who had come into the world while Corsica still belonged to the Genoese, Napoleon Buonaparte was born a Frenchman.

Three months earlier, in Dublin, the Earl of Wesley had celebrated the birth of his sixth child, Arthur, the future Duke of Wellington. In the years to come, Arthur Wesley, or Wellesley as he was often called, played an important part in the life of Napoleon Buonaparte.

The Corsicans were proud of their large families. Like the famous Roman matron, Letizia Buonaparte looked on her children as her jewels. She was to have thirteen, but only eight lived to grow up. Besides Joseph and Napoleon there were Lucien, Elisa, Louis, Pauline, Caroline, and Jerome. Of these Corsican children one was to be an emperor and the others would be kings and princesses.

The scrawny little Napoleon with the large head worried Letizia. "He is not sick, he eats well, yet he does not thrive," she complained. "He likes to be alone and when the boys tease him he flies into a temper. Then he'll fight brutes twice his size. The funny thing is, he always wins. No wonder! When he's angry there's a devil in him."

Napoleon used to roam the forests with Joseph and Lucien and swim in the sea. But most of all he loved to climb alone to the fort of Ajaccio where the Genoese had left behind many signs of their earlier power. Among these was a large cannon

made of bronze which the weather had turned to a spotted, shiny green. Napoleon would climb it and, sitting astride it, would stare out across the water toward the continent of Europe.

The teacher at the parish school where Napoleon studied with Joseph told his pupils about the different nations. There was Italy, home of Napoleon's ancestors. It was largely ruled by the Austrians, whom the Italians hated. There was

7

the kingdom of France, where new and dangerous theories were being written about by men who did not believe that kings had a special God-given right to rule. There was Spain, old and decaying, whose kings and queens were more often than not insane. Yet they owned not only the Spanish peninsula, except for Portugal, but nearly half of the New World. Then there was Great Britain. Although not very large, she was a powerful country, with possessions in the New World, too. But now the American colonies were giving her a great deal of trouble because they wanted to be free.

After Corsica fell Charles Buonaparte made the best of things and found a job with the French government. Once he was sent to France on a mission to King Louis XVI who gave him some money to start a mulberry plantation on the island. But Charles Buonaparte, who was vain and thoughtless, spent most of the money on fine clothes. He also brought back a lot of exciting news.

"There was an American at the Court, a man called Franklin," said Charles. "He is a scientist, I think, because he spent most of his time at the Academy of Sciences. He is working on—what was it?—electricity. But I found out what he really came for."

Little Napoleon's sea-green eyes looked as large as saucers in his thin face. "Tell us, Papa. What did he come for? Was it for the revo—revolution?" He got the long word out proudly.

Charles Buonaparte gave him a startled look and then turned to his wife. "This little pitcher has very large ears," he said. "Where did you learn that big word, Napoleon?"

"The teacher told us, at school. He says it is a bad thing, and that if the Americans make one, they are going against God. Didn't he say that, Joseph?"

"He said it is a bad thing because God made kings to rule," said Joseph.

"Is it wicked to want to be free?" asked Napo-

9

leon. "When I grow up I shall make a revolution in Corsica and drive out the French."

"Hush, there, boy!" said his mother sternly. "Do you want to get your father into trouble? Eat your bread and be quiet. Go on, Charles. What did the American come for?"

"He came to ask help for the Americans— money, troops. Mr. Franklin talked well and the King agreed to help. Not, I must admit, because he loves the rebels across the ocean, but because he hates the English across the Channel."

"He's playing with fire, the King," said Letizia. "And he who plays with fire is sure to get burned." She stopped and stared at her son. "Why is that child choking again? Napoleon! What's the matter with you? Our Lady give me patience!" she cried, throwing across the table to her husband a piece of coarse, dark bread which she had snatched from Napoleon. "Eating soldier's bread again! I can't get flour white enough for my baking, and he disgraces me by eating black bread!"

"How long has this been going on?" asked the father. "Where did you get that dog's fare? Answer me, Napoleon."

"It's not dog's fare! It is what the soldiers eat," said the boy defiantly.

"If it's for the soldiers, how do you come to have it?"

The boy was silent.

"Answer me—where do you get it?" insisted the father.

"He gives Mama's white bread to the soldiers," said Joseph, "and they give him some of theirs."

Napoleon shot him an angry look. His thin pale face reddened, a bad sign.

"Be quiet, Joseph," broke in Letizia. "Let Napoleon speak for himself. I want no son of mine to tell tales on his brother."

Joseph, shamefaced, was silent as his mother spoke to Napoleon. "Son, why do you give away my good white bread? Heaven knows we can ill afford it."

"I don't give it away!" Napoleon interrupted, his voice trembling. "I only exchange it for the soldiers' bread."

"Does it taste better than my bread?" she asked.

"No, Mama. In fact, I do not like it. But since I am going to be a soldier, I want to get used to soldiers' bread."

"Our Lady watch over him!" exclaimed Letizia, raising her eyes to the ceiling.

# [2]

## The Young Lieutenant

THE WOLF OFTEN CAME SCRATCHING AT THE
Buonapartes' door. With so many mouths to feed
and so little money coming in, Charles Buonaparte
decided to put his French friends to good use. Perhaps what Napoleon had said about becoming a
soldier gave him an idea. With the help of the
French governor of Corsica, Charles applied for
scholarships for his two eldest sons, Joseph and
Napoleon.

Late in December, 1778, he set out with them
for France. Joseph was placed at a school in Autun
where he was to study for the Church. As for

13

Napoleon, he was taken to the military academy at Brienne. Since the school admitted only young noblemen, Charles Buonaparte armed his son with the necessary papers. So when the boy signed the register he wrote: "Monsieur Napoleon de Buonaparte." The name was to undergo many changes. The first was the dropping out of the *u* to make the name easier for the French.

But to his schoolfellows Napoleon was a foreigner. They made fun of his peculiar first name. They laughed at his French. He looked so different from them with his keen, flashing eyes, his skin tanned by the Corsican sun, and the reddish-brown hair that fell untidily over his forehead. He was still fiercely Corsican and he let everybody know it.

"If you Corsicans are so brave, why did you let us beat you?" the French boys taunted him.

"You wouldn't have beaten us if it had been a fair fight. But you came ten to one," he shouted

back. "Four to one, we would have beaten you. Yes, even five to one."

"That's what you say. But we'd have won anyway."

"One of these days, you'll see!" Napoleon warned. "I'll go to Corsica with an army and drive out the French."

"You? Little *Paille au Nez?*" they jeered, making fun of his smallness and his name.

"Yes, I, Napoleon!" he yelled. "I'll do you French all the harm I can. I'll make you suffer for this!"

Brienne was very different from Ajaccio. Napoleon missed the sunlight and the sea. He shivered with cold. He hated the discipline and the small, bare cells where the pupils were locked in at night like so many prisoners. But he loved to read and study, which did not make him any more popular with his schoolmates. He made himself an arbor in the garden and there he would go with his books. He read everything he could find on geography and ancient history. In his imagination he fought famous battles all over again and won. He was the noblest Roman of them all and the bravest of Greek heroes.

He had a wonderful memory. Later, when he became famous, he used to say that his mind was like a cabinet full of pigeonholes in which he tucked away everything he wanted to remember. But he kept notebooks, too. On the last page of one of these, he wrote down a curious piece of information: "St. Helena. A small island on the Atlantic. An English colony."

He spent five years at Brienne. When he left the school as one of the King's cadets he was an awkward boy of fifteen. He was still small for his age, but his piercing eyes and his serious expression made people notice him. He spoke well and he always had something to say, for the pigeonholes of his mind were crammed full of knowledge.

His father, who had come to France for his health, was very proud of him. "Napoleon will be the head of the family," he said.

It was a great compliment to Napoleon who, after all, was a younger son. But his brother Joseph was the first to step aside for him.

Although Napoleon was the King's cadet he was still loyal to Corsica. At Brienne everybody had been used to his love for his homeland. But when he entered the Military School in Paris and talked loud and long about freeing the island, the students did not like it at all. Scarcely a day passed without a fight.

"You ought to be ashamed of yourself," a well-meaning friend scolded him. "You're about to become a French officer. You should bear this in mind and not talk so much about your love of Corsica. After all, isn't it part of France?"

A few months before his graduation Napoleon learned of his father's death. He was deeply grieved but he would not show his sorrow. He was also very much worried, for his father had left very little money. Joseph had no profession. The other children were all too young. The father had been right: from now on Napoleon would have to look after the family.

He felt the responsibility keenly when, right after his sixteenth birthday, he left the Military School as second lieutenant and went to his first post. At home his mother, to whom he sent part of his pay, was very proud. It was the first time that a

Corsican had received a commission from the Paris Military School, and that Corsican was her son.

Napoleon's feelings were still confused. He was wearing a French uniform. He was working with French soldiers. Yet he was troubled by strange dreams. In them Corsica, in the shape of a beautiful woman, would hold out a dagger to him, crying: "You must avenge me!"

But how could he avenge her? His blue and red coat with silk shoulder tufts was paid for by Louis XVI. He was in the service of France. Still, the idea of becoming Corsica's liberator gave him no rest. Because he could do nothing about liberating the island, he began to write its history.

Some time later he met the Corsican leader whose lieutenant his father had been. He showed him parts of the history. The general handed it back to him.

"You must make history," he said to him, "not write it. For you are like a man out of Plutarch."

The young lieutenant felt as if fate had spoken. A man out of Plutarch! That's what the general had called him. A man like the heroes and conquerors about whom the great Greek biographer had written! A man like Alexander the Great and Julius Caesar!

But people called him other things. Some said he was a madman, some that he was too ambitious. One thing he knew: he was very poor. Many times he had to choose between something to eat and the warmth of a reading room, which cost about the same. When his uniform began to wear out and his boots looked much too large for his thin legs, a little girl whose parents he used to visit, gave him still another name, Puss-in-Boots. It was quite ridiculous, after being called a man out of Plutarch.

He longed for something to happen so that he could make the world take notice of him.

# [ 3 ]

## *Revolution*

THAT SOMETHING HAPPENED. IT WAS THE FRENCH Revolution.

Of course, like a pot that finally comes to a boil, France had been feeling the heat long before 1789, the date that is usually given as the beginning of the Revolution. It had begun much earlier in the century when thinking people started asking questions about rich and poor, about those with power and those without.

All over Europe the poor struggled to break the chains that despots had put upon them. When the American colonies rebelled successfully against

England the people in France were filled with hope. Perhaps they too could free themselves of a tyranny that had lasted for centuries. Who knows —maybe the spark that kindled the French Revolution was lighted when Louis XVI sent help to the American colonies. He had done it much against his will, and in order to get even with England. And now, just after George Washington's inauguration in America, the French monarchy was in danger.

Dickens, in *A Tale of Two Cities*, tells what things were like at that time in England and France: "It was the best of times, it was the worst of times, it was the age of wisdom, it was the age of foolishness . . . it was the spring of hope, it was the winter of despair. . . . There were a king with a large jaw and a queen with a plain face on the throne of England: there were a king with a large jaw and a queen with a fair face on the throne of France. In both countries it was clearer than crystal to the lords of the State preserves of loaves

and fishes, that things in general were settled forever."

The American Revolution gave the throne of
England a terrible jolt. The French Revolution
threw down the throne of Louis XVI altogether.
Both Louis and Marie Antoinette, the queen with
the fair face, lost their heads on the guillotine. The
whole world was shocked by these brutal events,
but it should not be forgotten that the French
Revolution brought about much that was good.

At first the Revolution was in the hands of what
we now know as the middle class. Led by Mira-
beau, it rose up against the king and queen, who
stood for tyranny and injustice. Then a more violent group came into power. They wanted to
make a clean sweep of the old system. They did
away with the privileges of the monarchy and
they took over the property of the Church. They
also tried to abolish God and make the people
worship Reason instead. On the good side, they
wrote the Declaration of the Rights of Man, which

was to them what the Declaration of Independence is to us.

When the other rulers of Europe saw what was happening in France they began to fear for themselves. So the King of Prussia and the Emperor of Austria got together an army to overthrow the French Revolution. They drew into their armies the French nobles who had fled their country at the first sign of violence. It was the aim of Prussia and Austria to put a king back on the French throne. Otherwise they felt that no monarch in Europe would ever be safe.

This act on the part of two foreign nations only made the revolutionists fight the harder. Fearing that the nobles and the king's men who were still in France might work against them, they started what is known as the Reign of Terror. They set up the guillotine and began cutting off the head of everyone they thought dangerous to the Republic.

Altogether they put to death about five thousand anti-revolutionists. It was the act of a desperate people fearful of having their newly won freedom taken away from them. Indirectly it was to lead to their losing not only their freedom but also the Republic they were so proud of.

The Reign of Terror ended in the summer of 1794, and in 1795 Napoleon Bonaparte came on the scene again. Although he was now a brigadier general, he was as poor, as shabby, and as unkempt as ever. In his worn boots and frayed uniform he wandered about the Paris streets. He was devoured by ambition and angered at seeing men with half his ability getting ahead of him. Not that he had been lazy about making his way! In Corsica, three years earlier, he had attempted a bold stroke to seize power, but he failed and was banished. His whole family, too, had to flee the island.

This defeat made him give up any further idea of freeing Corsica. He became an ardent Republican. While fighting for the Republic he did so well that he came to the attention of the government in power and was given several important

*Thousands were beheaded at the guillotine*

commissions. At present, however, he was idle, out of sorts, and with little hope of bettering his condition.

All of a sudden the Royalist sections of Paris rose up against the Convention, the body of Republicans who governed France. The general who was sent to subdue the rioters fled before them. Within a few hours the rioting had become something much more serious.

The Convention met hurriedly to face the danger. It was a very ticklish matter. Frenchmen would have to be called upon to shoot down Frenchmen, and no one in the Convention wanted to commit himself by making such a suggestion. The peril was growing greater every moment. At last the names of some generals who could put down the rebellion were mentioned. Among them was heard the name of Bonaparte. Perhaps because it was not a French name, perhaps because the young general was already well known for his military talent, Barras, the head of the Convention, ordered: "Go and fetch this Bonaparte."

As it was, Bonaparte had been loitering about the Tuileries where the Convention was meeting. He had no love for the Convention because he knew the bad reputation of the men in it, especially Barras. Therefore when Barras told him: "Crush this Royalist uprising and I'll make you second in command of the army," he asked for time to think it over.

This was the chance he had been waiting for. Corsica had cast him out. His whole future depended on the way he would decide.

"I accept the offer," he said at last to Barras.

It was the 13th Vendémiaire according to the Revolutionary calendar, and the 5th of October, according to our own, when Napoleon Bonaparte led his forces against the Royalists. The previous night he had placed cannons and guns where he felt they were most needed. In the morning the battle began in the streets of Paris. By evening Bonaparte's men had mowed down with grapeshot the ringleaders of the Royalists on the steps of the church of Saint-Roch. The rest gave up and fled.

The Convention thanked its lucky stars.

Overnight the man who had been almost unknown the day before became a hero. He had saved France. "Bonaparte!" the people cheered when he passed by in the carriage which the Convention gave him to suit his rising fortune.

The Convention gave him much more, for Barras knew that Bonaparte would repay the gifts with interest. He was made a major general, and shortly afterward he became Commander in Chief of the Army of the Interior. What the Convention meant to say by rewarding him in this manner was: "You are anxious for fame and glory. Go and conquer Europe and make it into another French Republic. We shall all be the gainers."

Soon plans were made for the liberation of Italy from the Austrians, a polite way of saying that

France was going to invade that rich and beautiful country. Bonaparte was chosen to do the "liberating" and was named Commander of the Army of Italy. As the final reward, he was married to a lovely widow with two children, the ex-countess Josephine Beauharnais.

Two days later Bonaparte set out for Italy.

# [4]

## Food for Powder and Nothing Else

MEANWHILE, WHAT OF ARTHUR WESLEY, OR Wellesley, who was to play such an important part in the life of Napoleon Bonaparte? Was he too rising to fame and glory?

Far from it. While Europe was ringing with the name of Bonaparte who had done as great a thing as Hannibal by crossing the Alps with a large army, no one had ever heard of Arthur Wellesley. While the victories of Millesimo and Arcola and Rivoli were adding to the glory of the young Republican general, Arthur Wellesley's family despaired of doing anything with this dull member of their house. What made matters worse was that Arthur's brothers, William and Richard, were becoming famous as scholars and statesmen. They frequently felt it necessary to apologize for Arthur, who played the violin instead of making a successful career for himself.

Lady Mornington, his mother, had always shaken her head over this problem child. He had had the best advantages of his social class, private tutors, and an expensive education at Eton. From these he had gained nothing at all. As a last resort the family thought of training him for the church, but Latin and Greek were not for him.

"I'm afraid," said Lady Mornington rather heartlessly, "he is food for powder and nothing else."

Therefore, to prepare him for a career in the army, he was sent to a military school at Angers, in France. He remained there for two years.

The city of Angers, before 1789, was not like Paris, alive with revolutionary ideas. Angers was conservative, religious, and very loyal to the king, which meant very loyal to things as they were. The nobles were not showy and extravagant like those in the king's court. They lived simply and decently on their small incomes and they had a high sense of honor. Arthur Wellesley respected them and formed his character from what he saw. In other words he became conservative, aristocratic, and possessed of a strong sense of right and wrong.

When he returned home a young man of seventeen, he was as embarrassing as ever to his family, most of all to his brother Richard in Parliament. What could be done with a fellow who did not seem fit for anything? Richard took the matter into his own hands. Since he had good connections, he decided to use them.

"There is a younger brother of mine," he wrote to the Lord-Lieutenant of Ireland. "He is here at this moment and perfectly idle." Could the Lord-Lieutenant get him a commission? Any commission, so as to have him out of the way as soon as possible?

The Lord-Lieutenant of Ireland was eager to oblige his friend in Parliament. In March of 1787 Arthur Wellesley became Ensign, then a rank just below that of Lieutenant, of the Seventy-Third Foot, or infantry. He was under orders to go to India. It was a better stroke of luck than Brother Richard had expected.

But the newly made ensign did not go to India,

for he received a commission in another regiment. It was not until 1794, while England was helping Austria in the war against France, that Arthur Wellesley, Lieutenant Colonel by this time, first came under fire. He was given as his first task the command of what remained of the British forces which had been trying to hold the line of the Waal River in the Netherlands against the enemy French.

When the British army of twenty-five thousand soldiers had crossed the Channel, one hundred and fifty thousand Frenchmen were waiting for them. Austria's scant fifteen thousand still left the Allies very much outnumbered. From the beginning the battle had been nothing but a retreat for the Allies, who were under the supreme command of a son of King George III. The Austrians, seeing how things were going, decided to leave the English to themselves. After several months of skirmishes, Lieutenant Colonel Wellesley and his three battalions were almost the only defenders of the Waal line.

Winter now set in. Wellesley's soldiers, not one of whom had an overcoat, shivered in the snow. Then the food supply began to fail. Cold, hungry, and ill, the men died like flies.

"If we are not relieved there will be very few remaining shortly," Wellesley complained.

No relief came. The royal Commander in Chief not once showed his face among Wellesley's soldiers. Everyone seemed to have forgotten them —everyone but the French, who kept them in constant alarm by sudden attacks.

In the bitter cold the Waal froze. The French seized their chance and crossed the ice. Wellesley was forced to retreat. He had not changed his clothes for weeks. He had scarcely had a night's rest. With his men he fled in advance of the French so that at least he could save the lives of his soldiers. Every morning, after a bivouac on the icy fields, the ground was black with men and horses frozen to death.

When the men reached the port to sail back to England, they looked like an army of skeletons. Of the original forces that had crossed the Channel, only six thousand crossed it back again.

The young Lieutenant Colonel was shocked by this terrible experience. He had done his best, but unlike Bonaparte he had won neither fame nor glory. He might just as well have stayed at home. He was so discouraged that he decided to give up active military service and try for a government office instead. Without waiting for his successful brother to speak for him, he applied to the Lord-Lieutenant of Ireland. Perhaps he was not as smooth a talker as Brother Richard. Anyway, nothing came of his application nor of several others that he made.

The months passed and he felt more and more discouraged. He had no money. Moreover, he was sick of a fever that he had caught in the Netherlands. With every door shut against him in England, he wondered whether it might not be better

for him to try his luck in one of the colonies. Just then, as if by some joke of fate, he got his promotion. He was now a full Colonel in command of the Thirty-Third Foot.

He was once more in active service, but not in Europe, where the most tremendous war for empire which the world has ever known had just begun. He was to go with his regiment to India.

Illness kept him from sailing with his men, who left on the East Indian transport ships. But he caught up with them on a frigate at the Cape of

Good Hope. In February of 1797, while Napoleon Bonaparte was enjoying the fruits of his conquest like a king in an Italian palace, Colonel Wellesley reached Calcutta. Had he died then, nobody would even remember his name.

# [ 5 ]

## *More Worlds to Conquer*

WHILE NAPOLEON BONAPARTE WAS PLANNING TO make republics out of the Italian duchies taken from Austria, the French Republic itself was changing. It was now under the rule of the Directory, which was made up of five members. The chief of them was the sinister Barras from whom the young general had received the Italian command.

Barras, an ex-count, had lost none of his old tastes and for that reason tried to appear more republican than the rest. But the people were not fooled. When they saw the entertainments that were held in the royal palaces and the luxury that surrounded the Directors, they called them the Five Majesties. It was thought quite funny when the five Directors appeared publicly in their gold and velvet costumes, wearing pointed shoes and hats waving with plumes.

England, of course, was quick to ridicule the new government, and the English magazines were filled with verses making fun of the Directors. In one of these verses a Frenchman was supposed to say:

> *"God bless old England's gracious king*
> *Who blessed peace to us will bring.*
> *'Tis true that we are blessed with Five——*
> *Ah, had we now but one alive!"*

The French themselves noticed that something was happening to the Republic. Its slogan was still Liberty, Fraternity, Equality, as they could see in big letters on the walls of public buildings. Perhaps the people did have liberty. Perhaps they were all brothers and, maybe, they were all equal. But there were still the rich and the poor. Under the Directory a loaf of bread was as hard to get as under Marie Antoinette, who had said when the people complained that they had no bread: "Let them eat cake."

The Directors and their friends did not seem to lack anything, however. Their wives were rosy and well fed; they were dressed in silks and wore gold jewelry in their ears, on their arms, and about their ankles.

Where did all that luxury come from? From the State treasury—though the people did not know it. As a matter of fact the Directors were worried. They had promised many millions to Bonaparte's soldiers when they returned victorious, but there was absolutely nothing left to give them. The Directors were also worried about what to do with their large army that would be unemployed, now that Bonaparte was going to make peace with Austria.

"Let the soldiers plant cabbages," said Barras with a harsh laugh, adding, "if there are cabbages to plant."

In the midst of their worries, the Directors suddenly beheld a stream of treasure flowing in from the conquered states of Italy. They gasped in amazement. There were beautiful paintings by the greatest Italian artists—Leonardo da Vinci, Raphael, Titian. There were statues by Michelangelo and priceless masterpieces by the famous goldsmith, Cellini. There was also a bronze quadriga, a noble group of four horses that had adorned the entrance of St. Mark's cathedral. The quadriga had been a trophy of war many centuries earlier, and stood for Venice's greatness and splendor. Now it belonged to France.

These were all splendid gifts, but what made the Directors exclaim was the vast amount of money that arrived to help the government with its financial troubles. Barras congratulated himself on his choice. He had known Bonaparte would be good.

But the Commander in Chief was proving himself to be a wonder worker.

Not only Barras, but everybody else—with the exception of Austria and England—thought so, too. Ever since the outbreak of the French Revolution England had foreseen a serious problem in France. Now it saw a bigger problem in Bonaparte. It is true the young man had started out with lofty ideas of freeing downtrodden peoples. But had he been sincere? Even if he had been, might he not soon begin to think so much of himself that he would want to win the whole world? History had known ambitious men of that sort. While gaining fame and power for themselves they left behind them a trail of blood and destruction.

England was certain that Bonaparte would not stop at this first victory. Besides, the greedy Directors would not let him. They knew how easy it had been for Bonaparte to take the Italian states; the people had really believed that he came to free them.

"People of Italy!" he had addressed them. "The French army has broken your chains! France is the friend of all the peoples in the world! Come and welcome us."

And the Italians had welcomed the conqueror with open arms. Not only that. Other small nations which suffered under old and unfair systems now saw hope for themselves.

This, more than anything, made England fear for the future of Europe. England believed in legitimate governments and the monarchy. It hated violent changes brought about by revolutions. In Bonaparte's suddenly rising star it saw a threat to itself and to all Europe. It realized that from now on it had to stand against Napoleon Bonaparte and Republican France. Like the watchful leopard that was its symbol, England waited, ready to spring.

Meanwhile Napoleon was going from triumph to triumph. The dazed Austrians did not know which way to turn. They were used to the old methods of making war, and here suddenly was someone who had no regard for any of them.

A captured Austrian general lamented bitterly to the French officers: "You have a young jackanapes of a general who doesn't know anything about the rules of war. First he attacks us from the rear, then he comes on our left, then suddenly he moves on and does something else. It is preposterous! No wonder things are going badly with us! He goes against every tradition."

It was this originality of Bonaparte's that was to make him one of the most brilliant generals who ever lived. Europe was beginning to discover it, and so was the Directory.

All France was in a frenzy of joy when the hero returned from Italy. Crowds surrounded his house and filled the neighboring streets. They kissed one another, they wept, they cheered.

"Bonaparte! Bonaparte!" they repeated, as if they could not call his name enough.

At night under colored lanterns they danced in the streets. In the square where the old Bastille prison used to be, a plaster elephant as big as a house had been set up. It had a door that led inside, and huge legs like columns. All night long, young and old sang themselves hoarse as they galloped between the legs of the plaster beast. They did not know how to show their rejoicing over the man who had covered France with glory. Glory! Glory! With the name of Bonaparte the French said the word over and over like a charm.

Bonaparte went to some of the public ceremonies. How young he looked! How grave and modest in his plain uniform next to the Five Majesties in their velvet and feathers! He was like a personification of republican virtue.

He did not trust the Directors and he was right. While they were showing off the hero, they were wondering how to get rid of him and of his large, idle, restless army. In the speeches in his honor they hinted that there was another enemy to conquer, an enemy that hated the Republic, that ruled the seas, that was building up an empire in the East.

The hero of Italy, however, did not need their suggestions. "Europe is a molehill!" he would exclaim as he paced restlessly back and forth.

Like Alexander, he wanted other worlds to conquer. Also, like that ancient warrior, he turned toward the East. Egypt! He would carry republican ideals to the oppressed people of Egypt.

The truth was that his ambition gave him no peace. "Nobody remembers anything for very long in Paris," he said to a friend. "If I remain idle much longer I am lost."

The Directory was opposed to this expedition but was unable to prevent Napoleon from making it. He was too popular with the people. That was dangerous—for the Directory. So the wheels were set moving for the Egyptian expedition.

England heard, watched, and made ready.

# [6]

## Cairo and Abukir Bay

IT WAS MAY 19, 1798. AT TOULON HARBOR AND
at other points in France and Italy, Bonaparte and
his army were starting out for Egypt. The port of
Toulon looked as if another city, of decks and
sails, had sprung up out of the sea. Crowds that
had gathered from all parts clustered like bees on
the heights above the port to see Bonaparte em-
bark on the Admiral's ship, the *Orient*.

From a balcony Josephine Bonaparte looked
through her spyglass toward the *Orient*. She saw
her husband near the mainmast. He had his right
hand thrust in his waistcoat and he was gazing out

toward the open sea. She also saw the group of scholars, scientists and artists whom Bonaparte was taking along to make a study of Egypt. They were his Egyptian Institute.

Suddenly the cannon of the fort roared the signal. The cannon of the ships thundered their reply. The military bands struck up the songs of departure, and the crowds on the heights waved hats and scarves and shouted lustily.

The Admiral's ship bent her sails and pushed forward as the other vessels prepared to follow. But they were so jammed in the roadstead that for a while they strained like dogs on a leash. The people gasped; the *Orient* had begun to career! But she soon righted herself, spread her wings, and made for the open sea, followed by the rest of the fleet. The echo of the bands died down. The last sail disappeared on the horizon.

Once on his way, Bonaparte went like lightning, to the annoyance of Admiral Nelson, commander of the English fleet which had been on the lookout for him. However, a storm scattered Admiral Nelson's vessels, and by the time they got together again, Bonaparte had seized the island of Malta. Nelson then rushed eastward and scoured the Egyptian coast, but Bonaparte got past him without losing one vessel.

"The devil has the Devil's own luck!" cried Nelson.

It took Bonaparte six weeks to reach Alexandria, the Egyptian city founded long ago by Alexander the Great. His men had expected it to be grander than Italy and they were disappointed. There were no roads. Gone were the great theatres and temples that had once made Alexandria famous. Now and then a fallen column showed where the great city of the past had stood.

Before landing, Bonaparte had scattered far and wide copies of a proclamation which he had prepared at Malta. It was in several languages but the gist was the same. "Don't put up a fight because we, the sons of the great French Republic, come to deliver you from your oppressors. We are here to give you Liberty, Fraternity, and Equality."

In spite of these promises, a hail of cannon stones greeted the French liberators at the city gates. But after a few hours of struggle, Alexandria fell.

Bonaparte did not linger to celebrate his victory but went on to Abukir which protected one of the mouths of the Nile. In no time Abukir was his. Again he stayed only long enough to leave a governing body and then marched his army across the desert toward the Pyramids and Cairo.

It was a rugged march. The Arabs had filled the wells, the only water supply in all those miles of sun-baked desert, and many soldiers died of thirst. There were other hardships—the cruel heat and the treacherous attacks of the Arabs. The soldiers grumbled, for this was not anything like Italy, this broiling, desolate land. Bonaparte scolded his "children," as he called them, and tried to cheer them up with promises of great booty. Wasn't this the East of the wonderful *Arabian Nights?* What had Italy to compare with the wealth of the Orient?

Finally, after weary days, they saw the city of Cairo, all domes and minarets, rising up in the distance like something summoned by a magic wand. In the golden waste of sands, the immense Pyramids stood solid and eternal against a purplish light.

The ruling Beys of Cairo immediately sent out their Mameluke cavalry against Bonaparte. They were fierce fighters, the Mamelukes. When the French soldiers first saw them on their fleet Arabian horses, uttering strange cries as they brandished their curved, double-edged yataghans, they felt as if the fairy-tale Orient itself were charging against them.

They met in a series of skirmishes. The main battle, the Battle of the Pyramids, took place toward the end of July. As his army stood before him, forming its famous squares, Bonaparte looked at his men. They were about to meet in their first real conflict the dread, mysterious enemy. From them he turned his gaze on the Pyramids and then looked at his men once more.

"Soldiers!" he called to them, and his eyes flashed. "From the tops of those Pyramids forty centuries are watching you!"

He always knew the right thing to say to them at the right moment.

They fought as never before. Time and time again the Mamelukes dashed against the French squares and were pushed back by a bristling hedge of steel. They let out bloodcurdling yells of defiance. They hewed and slashed, cutting off many a Frenchman's head with their yataghans. For hours they returned to the charge until the wall of dead Mamelukes and horses rose higher and higher about the mighty squares.

The French then opened a running fire. The enemy fell by the hundreds. Seeing the battle lost, the Mamelukes finally rode off to the desert. Some tried to escape by crossing the Nile, only to drown.

*Many a soldier crammed his pockets with jewels*

After the battle Napoleon's soldiers dived into the river to retrieve the jewelled turbans of the Mamelukes. That night many a poor fellow had enough wealth to keep him in luxury as long as he lived—provided he did not leave his bones to bleach on the sands.

Bonaparte's success in so short a time seemed past belief. Malta seized from under Nelson's very nose! Egypt conquered in less than a month! No wonder the world began to believe in the star that guided Napoleon's destiny!

Bonaparte now settled in Cairo, in a sultan's palace. He was surrounded by all the luxuries of an eastern ruler and held a sort of court among the learned Saracen doctors and the potentates who had come to his side. Like any oriental Bey, he even had a Mameluke bodyguard, a dark-skinned youth named Rustan who was twice his master's size. Wherever Bonaparte went, Rustan, in his turban and embroidered costume, went too. At night he slept on the floor outside Bonaparte's door.

Once in Cairo Bonaparte started forming a government on the model of the French Republic. Little did he know, as he dictated the laws, what was happening in Abukir Bay where the French fleet had been confidently lying.

It was late afternoon of the 1st of August. Most of the French soldiers were in camp at Rosetta, not far from Abukir Bay. Suddenly they sprang up in alarm at the distant report of gunfire. They climbed to the fortress roof and looked through their telescope. A few miles away, but distinctly seen as well as heard, a naval combat was going on between the French fleet and Nelson's vessels which had at last caught up with their prey.

The French of Rosetta looked on helplessly. Dusk was gathering. Soon clouds of battle smoke covered the ships except where, for an instant, the darkness was gashed by the red lightning of gunfire. Three, four hours, the soldiers watched without being able to make out who had the advantage. Then a spreading flame, like a fan opening, lighted the bay. A moment later it was followed by a tremendous roar that shook the earth. One of the burning vessels had exploded, rocketing itself in flaming fireworks to the sky.

The fighting continued through the night and all of next day. On the morning of the third day there was a deathly calm.

The French gathered on the shores of Abukir to reckon their losses. The whole of the French fleet was destroyed. Admiral Brueys was dead, cut in two by a cannon ball. Another shot at the same instant had killed his heroic first captain, Casa-bianca. The *Orient* itself was no more. It was the dying burst of the Admiral's ship that the soldiers had witnessed from Rosetta. As far as the eye could see, wrecks lay like dead wood upon the water.

It was no comfort to Bonaparte when he heard the fatal news that Admiral Nelson had been badly wounded. The awful fact was that with the fleet destroyed he had no means of getting back to Europe.

"Well," said Bonaparte to his army, "we either leave our bones here, or we shall come out of it greater than the heroes of old."

He gave the soldiers no time to brood. Sending one of his best generals with a force to subdue Upper Egypt, he marched with the rest of the army to Syria.

Again he won victory after victory. But the important city of Acre held out stubbornly. For three months Bonaparte pounded at its gates in vain. Then one day a fleet of some thirty cruisers appeared in the distance. They were English cruisers, bringing help to the besieged city of Acre.

The French had succeeded in reaching the top of the rubble pile that had once been the wall of Acre. Some went down to the other side, but the ruling Pasha's men struck off their heads with their scimitars and laid them in a heap at the feet of their ruler. Soon the newly landed English troops came pouring in through the narrow streets.

Napoleon gave up the siege.

"Had Acre fallen," he said gloomily, "I would have had Constantinople. I would have had the Indies. I would have changed the face of the world."

England had prevented it.

Now a more dreadful enemy, the plague, attacked the French. They could brave a living foe, but before the deadly, unseen enemy they quailed with terror. Within a week the hospital tents were overflowing with the sick, many of whom were forced to lie outside in the cruel sun.

Napoleon at once began a retreat to Egypt. Hundreds were spared the hardship of that march by dying at Acre. The miles of desert were strewn with corpses. But when those who were left reached Cairo, they entered it with music and a great show of captured colors.

Bonaparte smarted under his defeat. "Ah, Acre! Acre! You have ruined me!" he would suddenly exclaim.

He decided to return to France. For more than six months he had received no news, thanks to the English who seized all the packets, and he had been away for more than a year. True, he had Egypt, a grand prize in any case. But, but——

"I've got to get back to France, English or no English!" he said with decision. "They're planning to catch me. Well, I'll give them a fair chance."

Leaving Cairo in charge of one of his generals, he started out for the seacoast with some members of the Egyptian Institute and a small army. The Institute was taking home many valuable notes of their explorations in science and in archaeology. The artist, Denon, had made hundreds of careful drawings not only of Egyptian art but of everything that would increase Europe's knowledge of the East. This valuable material was to appear in a work on the Egyptian expedition.

The French, however, never took back with them one of their most important finds, a large,

heavy slab of blackish stone carved with writing in three different languages. They had found it at Rosetta and had left it in Alexandria to send home later. But the English got it when Alexandria capitulated. It was the famous Rosetta Stone which made it possible for students to find the key to the reading of the Egyptian hieroglyphics.

A week after leaving Cairo, Bonaparte was on the outskirts of Abukir, which was now in the hands of the Turks. It was night when he approached the fortifications, but the moon was shining. When the sleeping Turks started up at the tramp of the marching French columns, Bonaparte had already given the order to attack.

The battle began at dawn, the Turks rushing out by the hundreds, by the thousands. Yelling fiercely, Turkish cavalrymen threw themselves upon the French, only to be beaten back. All morning long the fighting lasted; with every hour the Turks were pushed back farther and farther till they were hemmed in by the sea on the point of the peninsula.

By late afternoon the Turks were completely routed and thought only of saving their lives. In the wildness of despair they plunged with their horses into the sea in an effort to reach the English cruisers—three miles away!

That night the moon shone on a floating island of men and beasts, midway between the shore and the vessels they could not reach.

The loss of the French fleet had been avenged.

# [7]

## *First Consul—Then What?*

ON THE 11TH OF OCTOBER, 1799 THE DEPUTIES OF the French Assembly were listening with their usual boredom to a herald reading the bulletin. All of a sudden they started up, electrified. "Citizens!" the herald read. "The Directory is pleased to inform you that two days ago General Bonaparte landed in France——"

That was all they needed to hear. In a body they rushed out into the streets.

"Bonaparte is back! Bonaparte is in France!"

Instantly the news traveled to every corner of Paris, which turned itself inside out, for the houses could not contain the people and their joy. "Bonaparte is back! *Ca ira!* Everything will go well again," they greeted one another.

As it was, things had gone very badly under the corrupt Directory. Money and cabbages were scarcer than ever. What was much worse, the rich Italian conquest had been recaptured by the Austrians and their allies.

While Bonaparte was away the people had been longing for him to come back. They were tired of the Directory and wanted a change. The Directors had known the people's feeling all along and wished Bonaparte would die so that they could remain in power. Several times they had even spread the rumor that he was dead. Now here he was, quite alive and sure to ask for a reckoning.

And he did. With his brothers Lucien and Joseph, and a few others whom he let into the plot, he planned what is known as a *coup d'état*, a way of bringing about a sudden change in the government. The plotters were in a good position to do this. Bonaparte had the army behind him. Joseph had a good, level head, while Lucien was in a key position as President of the Five Hundred, the French Chamber. He was very young for such a high office, but his remarkable gift for oratory and his shrewd mind had won him his place.

In French history the day of the *coup d'état* is known as the 18th Brumaire—the 9th of November. It was a scheme of the greatest daring and one which only a man as popular with the people as Bonaparte would have attempted. For a long time the Republic had lived in dread of conspiracies. The bold plotters decided that at the meeting of the Council of the Ancients, set for the 18th of Brumaire, the members were to be warned of a dangerous plot to overthrow the government. Then, as soon as the Ancients had been roused to the proper alarm, Bonaparte was to be suggested as Commander of the Paris garrison for the protection of the nation. With this accomplished it would be easy to get rid of the Directory and to establish a new government with Bonaparte in charge.

Shortly after sunrise that fateful day, the garden and the street in front of General Bonaparte's house began to swarm with officers on horseback. The people who happened to be out wondered what was going on, but no one had the least suspicion of what was hatching.

Meanwhile at the Tuileries the Council of the Ancients opened their meeting at seven o'clock. No sooner were the members seated than one of Bonaparte's men began to fill the hall with warnings of the terrible danger that threatened the nation. "Daggers are drawn!" he shouted. "If the Council does not save France the Republic will cease to be and its corpse will be torn by vultures!"

This and many other things filled the shocked ears of the Ancients, who immediately passed a decree putting Bonaparte in command of the garrison. Losing no time, Bonaparte's henchman reported his success to the General, who set out for the Tuileries. By nine o'clock the palace yard was filled with Bonaparte's officers and the regiment of dragoons which he had picked up on the way.

He went at once to the Council chamber where he was greeted with cries of "Long live the Liberator!"

It was a good beginning. Nervously he took the oath. Then, in a choked voice, for he hated to make speeches except to his soldiers, he repeated the warning which the Ancients had already heard, and complimented them for passing the decree which would save the nation. "We want a Republic founded on Liberty and Equality!" he cried. "With the help of all lovers of liberty I shall save the Republic! I swear it in my name, and in the name of my companions-in-arms!"

"We swear it!" his officers echoed dramatically from the corridor.

His success was less brilliant at the Council of Five Hundred. But it did not matter since the two councils were meeting again at Saint Cloud in the morning.

During the night the Ancients and the Five Hundred had had a chance to think over the day's events. They became somewhat doubtful about the nation's danger. Some even suspected that the conspiracy was of Bonaparte's making. Bonaparte himself was very uneasy as he rode off to Saint Cloud next morning, and he heaved a sigh of relief when he saw the palace completely surrounded by his faithful grenadiers.

He had hardly entered the building when he heard a defiant "Long live the Republic!" instead of "Long live the Liberator!" To add to his dismay, he found that the two Councils were meeting in separate halls which meant that he would have to pass two ordeals.

After what seemed hours of waiting in an antechamber, before a fire that would not burn, Bonaparte was summoned to address the Ancients.

He entered in the midst of an angry discussion which became violent as it went on. When he got up to speak, he had barely opened his mouth before he was greeted with catcalls. Boldly he raised his voice and made himself heard, though he was extremely agitated. He had succeeded in winning over a good part of the house when someone called out: "What about the Constitution?"

"We have no Constitution!" he answered defiantly. "Each party in turn has trampled it underfoot. Let us save the foundations at least! Let us save Liberty and Equality!"

At these words shouts of approval came from the Ancients, who rose to their feet. Napoleon ended his speech to cries of "Long live Bonaparte," and then left to face the Five Hundred.

Out in the corridor his grenadiers surrounded him to lead him to the hall where the Five Hundred had been in session for some time. In spite of Lucien's efforts to quiet them they had stirred themselves up to a pitch of fury. As a result, the moment Bonaparte appeared he was deafened with cries of "Down with the dictator! Down with the tyrant! Outlaw him! Outlaw him!"

The grenadiers, whom he had ordered to remain outside, murmured with alarm. They heard Bonaparte raise his voice to speak. Then suddenly they saw him smothered by a group of angry council members who knocked him down and began pounding him with their fists. When the grenadiers saw the flash of daggers they broke through to their General and carried him off to safety.

In vain Lucien tried to restore order. With no respect for his office the council members dragged him down from his chair, repeating the cry: "Outlaw him! Outlaw Bonaparte and his accomplices!"

Lucien broke free. Tearing off his gown of office, he flung it aside dramatically and went out to the palace yard. He saw his brother on horseback among his grenadiers. Members of both councils had also rushed out into the yard where

a crowd had already gathered. Mounting his horse, Lucien joined Bonaparte.

The opportunity was too good for the rabble-rouser to miss. "Citizen soldiers! The Council of Five Hundred is dissolved!" he cried. "Assassins have taken over the meeting hall. They even talk of outlawing the General appointed by the Ancients to carry out their decree! As I am entrusted to execute their vote, I appeal to the arms of our warriors! Generals! Soldiers! Citizens! Save the representatives of the people from the representatives of the dagger!"

He paused and, drawing Bonaparte's sword from its sheath, pointed it at his breast. "Soldiers!" he said once more. "I myself would plunge this sword into my brother's heart if I knew it to harbor any thought against liberty."

There was a tumultuous shout. Lucien's oratory won the day for his brother.

Soon afterward the Council of Five Hundred broke up in disorder, the members scampering across the gardens to the threatening roll of drums. The Ancients met the same evening to set up the new government. It was to be a Provisional Consulate of Three, with Bonaparte as one of the Consuls. As he rode home at dawn he knew that his rise from now on would be rapid. Indeed, the other two Consuls offered little competition. On Christmas Eve Bonaparte was made First Consul— in other words, the head of the State.

He now moved himself and the government to the royal palace of the Tuileries and turned the former king's suite into his apartment and study. His wife Josephine had the gilt-painted chambers of Marie Antoinette. On the evening that they held their first reception for the representatives of other nations, the Tuileries was as brilliant as during the reign of the late monarchs. In fact, the court procedure was exactly the same.

Die-hard Republicans muttered, but they were won over by the reforms which the First Consul brought about, for he was an excellent administrator. There was nothing too trivial for his notice if he felt it helped France. When the Lyons weavers were not making any money, he advised Josephine and her friends to wear velvet. At once velvet became fashionable and the Lyons weavers thrived. He built roads and canals. He opened schools and museums. For that matter, he had brought enough treasures from Italy and Egypt to fill them!

Most important of all, Bonaparte worked with the best legal minds of his day on the system of law which is known as the Code Napoleon. It took a long time in the making, but it was an important and valuable work. The Code Napoleon was considered very revolutionary in the changes and reforms which it introduced. It provided that there should be no hereditary nobles. All the children in a family were to have an equal share in the inheritance, instead of having most of it go to the firstborn son, as used to be the case. In the courts of justice it made every person of whatever race or religion equal before the law. It introduced trial by jury and a public trial, instead of the secret and often unfair trials, which had been the rule under the old kings.

The Code recognized a civil marriage before the law, whereas earlier only a religious or church marriage was considered legal. It also provided for a legal separation between husband and wife when a marriage did not work out. There were dozens of provisions, covering every phase of life, and they did away forever with the injustices of the old system.

Bonaparte was so proud of this body of laws that he once said: "If I should ever be painted for future ages, I should like to be shown with the Code Napoleon in my hand."

No sooner was Napoleon in power than the Count of Provence, the brother of the guillotined king, demanded to sit on the throne. In fact he had begun calling himself Louis XVIII after the king's young son died in prison as Louis XVII. Bonaparte answered him very curtly. "You could not do so," he wrote, "without trampling upon five hundred thousand corpses."

Because of this the Royalists made several attempts to kill Bonaparte. Once he missed death by less than a minute when a bomb exploded on the

Rue Nicaise as he was on his way to the theatre in his carriage. Scores of innocent people were killed and it was a miracle that his wife, following him in another carriage, escaped.

Josephine, however, was still an aristocrat at heart and tried to make Napoleon bring back the monarchy.

"I wish you would listen to me, Bonaparte," she said to him one day. "Only this morning the Duchess of Guiche told me—and she had it from the Count of Provence himself—that if you make him king he will put up a column. On top of the column there would be a statue of you placing the crown upon his head."

"Fine! Fine!" Bonaparte agreed. "And under the pedestal would be my body!"

So two years went by. In the meantime he had crossed the St. Bernard pass with his army and reconquered Italy, adding the name of Marengo to the list of his victories. Treaties were made and broken and the sound of marching feet was heard

79

constantly all over Europe.

Then in 1802 Bonaparte was made Consul for life. He was now king in everything but name. But he was fated for more than kingship, and deep in his heart he knew it. For the present it was war, open war between France and England.

Meanwhile the man who was to play the most important part in the final duel was still in India, a minor hero in minor colonial wars. But Major General, the Honorable Arthur Wellesley, former governor of Mysore, would soon be returning to England. As Wellesley was preparing to leave Calcutta, Napoleon Bonaparte was about to shed his last name and become Napoleon, first Emperor of the French.

# [8]

## *Coronation at Notre Dame*

IT WAS THE FIRST DAY OF DECEMBER, 1804. ALL over the civilized world the talk was of one thing and of one person, the Coronation of Napoleon, which was to take place the following day. News did not travel quickly before the invention of the wireless telegraph. But everyone had known since May what was coming, for it was then that the French had voted to make their First Consul their Emperor.

Napoleon had been very modest about it at first, and had refused. But perhaps it was because they had originally suggested making him king. What novelty was there in that? France had had plenty of kings. But Emperor—that was another matter! There had never been an Emperor of France before. He accepted.

He sent a messenger at once to Pope Pius VII who was a mild, saintly man. His Holiness must come to Paris for the Coronation, wrote Napoleon. It would be a wonderful thing for His Holiness to do for him, the friend of religion. Had he not restored the worship of God which had been abolished by the French Revolution? And had he not made the church bells ring again after a long silence?

However, it was unheard of for a Pope to leave Rome to crown anybody, even Napoleon. Kings and Emperors had always come to the Pope. Still, His Holiness had to admit that Napoleon was right when he wrote: "This is one of the most important turning points in the history of the world."

Therefore, although the Cardinals grumbled that His Holiness was being treated like a lackey running to the command of his lord, the Pope set out for Paris. Who knows? Perhaps by this act he might bring about lasting peace.

Meanwhile Napoleon's family had flocked to the capital. With Napoleon's rise they too were climbing up. His three sisters became Princesses of the Blood, like the sisters of the ancient kings, and his brothers became Princes. Josephine's son Eugene and her daughter Hortense, who had married Napoleon's brother Louis, also received special honors. This annoyed the rest of the Bonapartes, for the clannish Corsicans hated Josephine, an outsider. Not that they had to fear being left out whenever gifts were distributed. Napoleon was more clannish than any other member of his family.

Still, they squabbled over ranks and titles. Among other things, the women objected because they would have to hold Josephine's train at the Coronation.

"But that's part of the Court procedure," Napoleon tried to explain. "It is always done. Besides, the Empress's mantle is so heavy that she could not take a step if someone didn't hold the hem."

The only way the women could be made to consent was to have their own trains held, too.

All day long, that first of December, the royal palace was like a madhouse. Tailors and hairdressers bumped into one another in their hurry to attend to the Princesses. At a huge table the painter Isabey was arranging dozens of small dolls inside a model of Notre Dame Cathedral. Each doll represented some imperial person or courtier who would be taking part in the ceremony. By glancing at the model, he would learn where he was to sit during the Coronation ceremony. It was easier for Isabey to work with dolls than with the quick tempers of some of the people he had to deal with.

When the great day dawned, it was cold and foggy. The ladies wrung their hands. Their beautiful clothes! How unkind of the weather! The streets, however, had started filling long before daylight. Never had there been such crowds, what with the Parisians who never missed anything, and what with foreign visitors who had taken over every hotel. People were now hanging out of windows which they had hired at fantastic prices.

Toward the middle of the morning the sky began to clear and the spirits of the crowd brightened with the sun. Solemnly the procession began to file out of the Tuileries. First came the Pope's retinue, headed by his chamberlain mounted on a mule, which made the people giggle. Then came His Holiness, seated in a carriage, blessing the people with his hand and his smile.

But it was the Emperor and Empress whom everybody wanted to see. Their crystal-and-gold carriage came at last, a curious, delicate thing like a large jewel box. The Emperor and the Empress glowed with precious gems. Napoleon, dressed in white velvet and a mantle of purple and ermine, wore on his plumed hat a diamond as large as a pigeon's egg. It was the famous Regent. Josephine, sitting beside him, was all in white satin embroidered with gold and silver. She was older than the Emperor, but she looked so young and so beautiful that everyone exclaimed in admiration. Then came Napoleon's Mameluke, making everyone shout with delight as he passed wearing a colorful native costume and riding an Arabian steed as splendid with jewels as its master.

It took over an hour for the procession to cover the short distance to Notre Dame. Within, the cathedral was a mass of gold and rich hangings. The Pope took his place on the throne before the altar, with his Cardinals in their red robes all about him. Napoleon waited on the steps with his courtiers, while Josephine stood a little below, surrounded by her ladies. He looked grave and majestic, but his pale face was paler than ever.

In the silence the organ suddenly pealed forth and a chorus of a hundred voices took up the solemn music. The Pope now moved about the altar where lay the crowns and the vial of holy oil. Slowly the Emperor and the Empress began to walk up the steps, followed by their court. All of a sudden Josephine reeled back and nearly fell. The Princesses, by an odd coincidence, had lost hold of her train at the same time. Napoleon darted them a terrible look, but His Holiness was waiting and he went up to the altar.

Chanting the Latin words of the ritual, the Pope anointed Napoleon with the holy oil that had given France her kings and now gave her an Emperor. As His Holiness was about to reach for the crown, Napoleon went past him, took it from the altar and, first raising it high, laid it upon his own head.

It was a bold thing to do, and everybody gasped in amazement. For before this, it was the Pope who had always crowned the kings. By his act Napoleon said that he owed the crown to his own achievements.

Josephine now went up the steps and knelt at

*Napoleon laid the crown upon his own head*

the altar, joining her hands as if in prayer. Napoleon lifted up her crown also, then placed it upon her bowed head.

"*Vive l'Empereur!* Long live the Emperor!"

The shout filled the cathedral and was taken up by the thousands outside.

It was several hours before the chanting and the music and the rest of the ceremony were over. Napoleon was bored after a while and stopped paying attention, thinking his own thoughts instead. At one point he leaned over and, tapping his brother Joseph on the shoulder with his sceptre, said in a loud whisper: "If only our father could see us now!"

Indeed! If only Charles Bonaparte could see his two sons who often had not had enough to eat! Now one was an Emperor. The other, thanks to the Emporer, would soon be king of the ancient Kingdom of Naples—after the Spanish Bourbons who occupied the throne were hustled out of it.

It was an amazing achievement, this Coronation

of Napoleon. From a childhood of poverty on a small island, he had risen in an age of trouble and strife to the highest rank a nation can offer.

The day he was crowned he was only thirty-five years old. The world looked at the wonder and marveled.

But Napoleon was not happy. Josephine's eyes filled with tears when she heard him murmur to himself, as he took stock of his great empire: "To whom shall I leave all this?"

For a king and, even more, an emperor, must have an heir. Napoleon had no children of his own.

# [9]

## Duel Between France and England

NAPOLEON HAD NOT BEEN LONG ON HIS THRONE when Sir Arthur Wellesley sailed for England from Calcutta. On the way he stopped off on the island of St. Helena which would one day play its part in the Emperor's life.

When Wellesley reached England he found the whole nation in a state of alarm. Beacon fires were kept ready along the Channel coast to send up warning flares. Britannia who ruled the waves was in danger of invasion by the French!

Wellesley, so long away, could hardly believe it until he went one day to call on the Secretary of State. In the waiting room he found a man whom he recognized at once from pictures that had reached him in Calcutta. The man had lost an arm in the service of England, and he showed the scars of many wounds. It was Admiral Nelson.

The Admiral had a long conference with the Secretary of State, and then returned to the waiting room, looking very grave. What had he talked about with the Secretary of State? Before long Wellesley and the whole English nation knew.

After the destruction of the French fleet at Abukir, Napoleon started building up another. Every shipyard in France had been kept busy for years. At Boulogne a camp for the soldiers who were to invade England rose up under the Emperor's supervision. He studied the currents and the winds of the English Channel and made note of the fogs. He called in experts for their advice. He was planning the very thing that the English boasted could never be done—an attack on their island. At last, in October 1805, Napoleon was ready and ordered his fleet to the Spanish waters where the King of Spain was sending his own ships to help.

On the 21st of October, Admiral Nelson found them at Trafalgar on the southwestern coast of Spain. He drew his fleet as close as possible to the enemy vessels and the engagement began. The English fired rapidly, aiming low at the flanks of the ships and causing enormous damage. The French, on the contrary, like the Spaniards, aimed at the masts, often wasting their shots. Within an hour two Spanish ships had surrendered. In another hour many of the French vessels were either sinking or burning. Still the firing continued, more violently than ever. Nelson wanted to make it impossible for Napoleon to threaten England from the sea again. By the end of the battle most of the French and Spanish ships had surrendered. The rest fled toward the Spanish port of Cádiz in a terrific storm.

The English pursued and caught up with them.

In the harbor of Cádiz, as the thunders of heaven mingled with the blasts of the cannon, the remainder of the unlucky fleet was either captured or destroyed. For weeks the people of Cádiz had the grim task of burying the bodies washed ashore.

It was not till November 7 that the news reached Paris. Napoleon was then fighting in Germany, so his minister Talleyrand had to break the news to him. After giving him the tragic details, Talleyrand closed with: "Alas! How could it be otherwise when our genius and our luck were in Germany?" The flattery did not make Napoleon's defeat any easier to bear.

England's victory was not all joy. Admiral Nelson was killed at Trafalgar.

From now on, no matter who was fighting whom in Europe, it was really a duel between France and England.

At present, in spite of the naval disaster, the duel was in Napoleon's favor. On the first anniversay of his Coronation he won the battle of

*At Trafalgar Nelson found the French fleet*

Austerlitz against Austria and Russia. This was one of his most famous victories. The day after Christmas, when the treaty was signed, his empire was larger by many hundreds of miles of territory.

He now sent his brother Joseph to rule over the Kingdom of Naples, and his brother Louis was made King of Holland. Then, to protect the French border, Napoleon did away with the German Empire and formed a league of friendly states along the Rhine, making himself their protector.

For the next few years there was no more powerful ruler in all Europe. England, however, kept watch over the sea. While Napoleon was enlarging his empire by cutting off slices of other kingdoms, or by taking them over altogether, England was sending her mighty navy with troops and supplies to Napoleon's enemies.

Napoleon became so drunk with power that he did not know where to stop. He made the very serious mistake of invading his former ally, Spain. True, Spain's king and queen were no credit to the nation. But the Spaniards had a strong patriotic feeling and rose up against the French. Instantly England came to Spain's help. While Britain's mighty navy guarded the coast, her troops and supplies poured into Spain, just as they had poured into Portugal when the French had driven out the Portuguese royal family.

Now Napoleon began having the unpleasant surprise of receiving bulletins which were not at all what he expected. "Wellesley has defeated General Laborde at Rolica," read one. Another said: "Wellesley has defeated Marshal Junot at Vimiera."

"Who the devil is this Wellesley?" Napoleon inquired angrily.

At last, sick of having his generals and marshals defeated on every hand, he himself went into Spain. He traveled in a magnificent blue-green carriage furnished like a private room, with a desk, bookcase, and even a folding bed. With his usual luck he defeated the Spaniards and entered the capital. The throne of Madrid was now his. What to do with it?

He might have given it to Lucien who had been so useful to him during the *coup d'état*. But they had quarreled and Lucien had gone to live in Rome. Jerome was still too young for such an important kingdom. Nevertheless, the throne must remain in the family. He therefore called Joseph away from Naples, gave the Neapolitan kingdom to his brother-in-law Marshal Murat, and seated the unwilling Joseph on the Spanish throne. The Bonaparte clan was taking over Europe.

# [10]

## The New Empress

IT WAS BY FIGHTING THAT NAPOLEON WON THE countries that were falling into his hands, and it was only by fighting that he was able to keep them. For he had to defend them not only against their patriots, but also against the other monarchs of Europe who feared the same fate as the dispossessed kings.

In May of 1809 Napoleon was besieging Vienna, the capital of Austria. Several times before, Napoleon had conquered Emperor Francis II and pushed him off his throne. He had signed treaties with the Austrian and come to terms with him.

But each time Emperor Francis had found allies to help him regain his throne.

This time Napoleon was very angry and wanted to crush Emperor Francis by taking his capital city, which the Austrians were defending with all their might against the French batteries outside their walls. The siege had been going on for days. Parts of the city were in flames. The smoke of the burning houses mingled with the smoke of battle, and cries of distress could be heard above the shooting. Yet the people still refused to yield.

Soon after the French had redoubled their fire, the city gates burst open and an Austrian officer bearing a flag of truce begged to see Napoleon.

"Sire," said the Austrian, "I do not bring you surrender. I come pleading for mercy. Your Majesty, throw down our walls if you must, but turn your batteries away from the imperial palace."

"Why so?" inquired Napoleon. "Your Emperor has fled. Whom do you wish to protect?"

"His child, Sire, is lying there ill——"

Napoleon scowled and gave the officer a piercing look. "I also know that the young prince is with him," said Napoleon. "You see, I am well informed."

"Sire, it is his daughter, the Archduchess Marie Louise. She is very ill. It was a question of moving her and thereby risking her life, or of trusting to Your Majesty's goodness of heart."

"It is very strange for a father to leave a sick child in a flaming city," said Napoleon. "This is some trick. I am sorry, but the imperial palace and the sick archduchess will have to take the same risks as the tenements and the shoemaker's children. Surrender, and you will be spared."

"Sire, you would not kill a helpless young girl!" the officer pleaded.

"I am sorry," Napoleon repeated, rising to end the interview. "A young girl?" he asked abruptly. "I did not know that Emperor Francis had a grown daughter."

"The Archduchess is just seventeen, Sire."

"That is strange," said Napoleon thoughtfully. Then he glared threateningly at the officer. "You swear this is no trick?" he asked.

"It is the truth, Your Majesty. Upon my honor," replied the Austrian.

"What a hard heart such a father must have," remarked Napoleon after the Austrian had gone. "Leaving a young girl to the horror of a bombardment!" And he gave the command to turn the guns away from the palace.

Emperor Francis and his allies were again beaten. But this time Napoleon himself nearly met defeat. So far the only battles he had lost were those which he had not personally commanded. This time, at Essling— But he did not like to think of it. It was enough that Emperor Francis signed another treaty and gave up some of his finest provinces to the French.

Napoleon was getting tired of the endless warfare. He was certain that if he had been an emperor by divine right the other rulers would have accepted him and left him in peace. But because he owed his rise to his own efforts they looked upon him as an upstart. There was one way of making the other monarchs recognize him. It was by marrying a wife of royal blood and obtaining an heir for his empire. Since his talk with the Austrian officer he had known who his next wife would be. But first he had to divorce Empress Josephine.

As it was, Josephine had long been living in dread of this very divorce. She knew that Napoleon owed it to France to leave an heir. It is true, he could have adopted her son Eugene and chosen him as his successor. But there was not a drop of Napoleon's blood in Eugene's veins and the people would not have been satisfied. They did not want any of Napoleon's brothers, either. But how they would welcome a son of the Emperor's to carry on the glory of France!

Knowing all this, Josephine could only submit when, after a struggle with himself, Napoleon

demanded the divorce. He loved Josephine, but he loved the empire more.

Josephine warned him, however, that he was making a dangerous mistake by marrying the Archduchess Marie Louise.

"She has been brought up to hate you," she said. "Do you think she will ever forget that you have driven her father from his throne again and again? Do you think *he* will ever forget it?"

Friends who dared to speak frankly to him told him the same thing, but he thought he knew better. A few months after he divorced the wife he loved, Napoleon married Marie Louise.

When he brought back his young bride to Paris the people dutifully cheered, but they were disappointed. They were used to Josephine's queenliness. The Austrian wife was a big, healthy-looking girl, very stiff and very self-conscious.

They admired her lovely blond hair and blue eyes, but they could get no response out of her. "She's just like a big, clumsy doll," commented one of Napoleon's sisters.

On the whole, however, the people were pleased with the marriage. The new Empress might not be all that they desired, but she would give them what they wanted—peace and, they hoped, an heir. They wondered whether she would ever forget that her great-aunt, Marie Antoinette, had lost her head on the guillotine. How times had changed! Now the Republic was an empire, and the First Consul the most powerful emperor of Europe. If only Marie Louise would give France an heir!

At the end of a fairly peaceful year, the people's wish was about to be granted. Napoleon could hardly contain his joy. In honor of the coming event the city of Paris sent a beautiful cradle to the palace, to receive the imperial heir. At least the people hoped it would be an heir and not an heiress. As a compliment to Napoleon, the Eagle, they had the artist who designed the cradle place a silver eaglet at the foot of it.

On the 20th of March, 1811, the people of Paris, who had scarcely slept a wink all night, listened eagerly as the cannon began to boom telling the world that an imperial child had been born. Silently they counted. At the twenty-second report they went wild with joy. Had the firing stopped at twenty-one, it would have meant that the Empress had borne a daughter. But the cannon boomed on and on, until it had fired one hundred and one times, which meant that the throne of France had an heir.

Napoleon's dearest wish, for himself and for the French empire, was now realized.

That same day the baby, who at birth had become the King of Rome, was privately baptized in a chapel of the palace. He was called Napoleon Francis Joseph Charles.

# [11]

## *The Snows of Russia*

THERE WAS NO ONE IN THE WORLD WHOM NAPO-
leon loved as much as he loved his son. Nothing
was too splendid for the little King of Rome. His
carriage, in the shape of a large gold scallop shell,
was drawn by a pair of trained deer. Before he
could even sit up he wore the broad ribbon of the
Legion of Honor, the highest decoration in the
realm. He had toy soldiers and drums and a hobby
horse so beautifully made that it almost seemed to
be alive.

Often, when the Emperor was working, he had
the King of Rome brought into his study. With

the golden-haired child in his arms, Napoleon re-arranged the map of Europe, making France larger and larger.

"Who knows?" he remarked to one of his secretaries. "Perhaps some day the crown on my son's head will bring together all the nations of the world. . . . Tell me, isn't he a fine-looking boy, my little son?"

No one could deny that. He was a beautiful child, with the hair and mouth of his mother and the fine brow and eyes of his father. He was also

109

very intelligent and, what pleased the Emperor most of all, he adored his father.

For nearly a year after the King of Rome's birth it really seemed as if the dove of peace had spread her wings over Europe. But it only seemed so. Spain, with England in the background, was still putting up a fight against France.

In the North, Russia, which for a time had been friendly to France, showed signs of going over to its former allies. But Napoleon was not worried. Surely his father-in-law would not join in a war against his own daughter's husband! But there was always England—France's most stubborn enemy from the time of the Revolution. England—and Russia. He must strike at them to protect his empire.

"I still believe that only by taking India can I cut off the life line of England. Russia will then be easy," he brooded. "I can see Moscow occupied and the Czar perhaps killed by the people—and I would acquire another throne. Then I could re-shape Europe for my son. The war clouds are gathering. The storm will break. But after that the sun will shine on a permanent peace."

In June of 1812 the storm broke as Napoleon opened the Russian campaign.

The French people were distressed. Napoleon's wars had taken so many men that now young boys, mere children, were being drawn into the army. The marshals did not dare complain, but they showed their disapproval of this new war by their lack of enthusiasm. Napoleon was too deep in his dream of conquest to take much notice.

England, however, was wide awake. With the Emperor's army now marching toward Russia, Wellesley—or Wellington as he was now called, was striking at Napoleon through Spain and Portugal.

Before the end of the summer the Emperor had crossed the Russian border. But where was the Russian army? Every day he hoped to catch up with Czar Alexander's forces, but he found only broken bridges and burned villages.

For weeks this game of hide-and-seek went on, without a single battle. Meanwhile the provisions were giving out. The starving horses that were to have fed on the green steppes of Russia were forced to eat the thatch of the huts along the way, and the men ate the horses.

Finally, at Smolensk, Napoleon caught up with the Russians. After three assaults the city fell. But when the French made ready to dash through the gates in search of food, they were pushed back by smoke and flames. The whole city was on fire.

Napoleon drove on in desperation. Every day, although no battles were fought, he lost thousands through the cruel forced marches, starvation, and sickness. Before Smolensk, as it was, he had already lost one hundred thousand of his army of half a million.

At last, at Borodino, Napoleon caught up with the enemy. If only they would fight he might have the decisive victory he needed to dictate his terms! This time the Russians agreed to a pitched battle.

Napoleon called for his muster rolls. While he was sticking colored pins into a map of the region, a courier galloped to his tent. Napoleon read the despatch without a word, but his face showed that it was bad news. Wellington again! This time he had defeated Marshal Marmont at Salamanca in Spain! The French had lost fourteen thousand to the five thousand casualties of Wellington and the Allies.

Silently he handed the despatch to his staff and went on mapping out the battle of Borodino.

"Tomorrow I'll probably be losing twenty thousand men," he said gloomily.

He was wrong. He won the battle of Borodino, but the price of victory was five times that amount.

By the middle of September he and his army reached the gates of Moscow. The French poured into the capital through one gate as Czar Alexander's soldiers retreated from the other.

"How strange," exclaimed Napoleon. "There's not a smoking chimney in all Moscow!"

Indeed, the city was like an empty shell. Not a soul came out into the streets. The churches and bazaars were deserted. When he entered the Kremlin, the palace of the Czars, he found it as silent as a tomb.

He had scarcely gone to bed when he was startled by a cry of "Fire!" Leaping up, he went to the windows where his staff joined him. The whole city was going up in flames in every quarter. As they looked on, new fires were starting up.

"What a terrible sight!" cried the Emperor. "What a people! To think of burning up their own capital!"

By a miracle the Kremlin escaped the flames. By another miracle, the soldiers found a great quantity of food and supplies in underground warehouses. The starving men ate and drank and for a time forgot their troubles.

It was the strangest victory that Napoleon had ever won. He was in a conquered city and he might as well have been in a graveyard. He was a

*A cry of "Fire!" startled Napoleon*

victor and yet Alexander would not admit defeat. In vain Napoleon let the precious days slip by, waiting for the Czar to agree to a treaty of peace. A flurry of snow fell late in September, a warning of what was to come. His marshals spoke of the danger of delay, but still the Emperor waited for a message from the Czar. It never came.

At last, on the 19th of October, Napoleon began his retreat from Moscow. Murat, all gold braid and plumes, opened the way with his brilliant cavalry. The bands played stirring marches and the soldiers fell into step. This was the hardest march of all, to outstrip the worst enemy they had ever faced—the Russian winter.

It came, earlier even than the Czar had dared to hope.

Men and horses died by the thousands during the icy nights. Hunger and the Cossacks killed thousands more. With their boots rotted away and their clothes in rags, the survivors at last reached the frozen Beresina River. It took them three days to cross it. When the ice broke up the following spring, twenty thousand soldiers of Napoleon's Grand Army lay dead at the bottom.

Of the proud half million who had set out for Russia, only nine thousand returned to France. It was the greatest disaster the world had ever known. And yet Napoleon had accomplished what he set out to do: he had taken Moscow—a city of ashes. France, where nearly every family was in mourning, had no cheers for this victory.

Napoleon had hardly embraced his little son when he was obliged to go to war again. Russia, uniting with Prussia, no longer feared the man who had been defeated by the White Winter. In Spain, meanwhile, Wellington had beaten King Joseph at the battle of Vittoria. It meant that Napoleon's power in the Spanish Peninsula was gone.

Napoleon himself, however, was still the genius of battle. In spite of the overwhelming numbers of the Allies, he crushed them everywhere and made them sue for a truce. While he was waiting in Dresden for the negotiations, he wondered what part Emperor Francis would play. Where would he stand if war were renewed against his son-in-law?

Napoleon had not long to wait for an answer. At the stroke of midnight, on August 10, 1813, a burst of rockets of different colors lighted the sky over Dresden. (In those days when the telegraph and telephone were unknown, this was the spectacular way in which armies communicated with each other.) By the color of one of the rockets, Napoleon knew that his father-in-law had joined the Allies and would be fighting against France.

Napoleon was not aware of Wellington's influence in making Emperor Francis come to his decision. Until the battle of Vittoria, the Austrian Emperor still thought he would be on the winning side if he stood by Napoleon. At the news of Wellington's victory, however, he joined the Coalition that was forming against his son-in-law.

# [12]

## The Turning of the Tides

IT WAS A SHOCK FOR NAPOLEON, EVEN THOUGH he had been prepared for it. A father who would leave a sick daughter in a bombarded city would take sides against that daughter's husband if he felt he could gain by it.

The city of Dresden had arranged for a festival on Napoleon's birthday. He changed it to a grand review of his army, as if to show the huge Coalition of nations against him that he still had his soldiers and his genius.

But he was worried. Every day he had another piece of bad news. Some of his own generals deserted and went over to the Coalition. Frenchmen were taking up arms against Frenchmen. He also heard that the enemy, strengthened by the might of England on land and sea, proposed to keep a combined army of a million men ready all the time, until he, Napoleon, had been crushed. A million men—and he had been able to raise only a few hundred thousand new soldiers! France was against the war and yet he must fight.

He fought small, teasing engagements around Dresden and won. September and part of October passed with no striking triumphs. All at once, the army of the Coalition, sweeping across Germany, began toppling over the little kingdoms that Napoleon had created. Bavaria surrendered. Westphalia threw over King Jerome Bonaparte and joined the Coalition. The tides of war that had swept everything before Napoleon now turned against him.

Toward midnight of October 16th, men of the French Army waiting before Leipzig saw three rockets of lightning-like fire streak up into the sky over the enemy camp. Then four blinding red rockets answered them a distance away. (The generals of the armies massed against Napoleon were exchanging the signals which meant that they were ready for the coming battle. By the colors of the rockets and by their number, the French could tell the nationality and the size of the enemy they had to face.)

"It means that tomorrow we fight a quarter of a million men," said Napoleon.

He had only half that number at his command.

He was very ill. As he groaned with pain his officers urged him to go to bed. "I cannot!" he cried. "A sick soldier can go to the hospital. A general dies standing."

The two armies met in the morning. But the sun set and still the fierce battle continued far into the night. Finally at a signal from the guns, both sides laid down their arms and the exhausted soldiers slept upon the ground. Daybreak saw the battle renewed, more desperate than before.

IRELAND

Dublin

ENGLAND

NETHER-LANDS

London

ATLANTIC

OCEAN

Waterloo

Leipzig

Boulogne

Paris

BAVARIA

FRANCE

ITALY

Toulouse

Cannes

Genoa

Toulon

Corsica

Rome

Madrid

Ajaccio

Elba

SPAIN

Sardinia

Cadiz

Sicily

Trafalgar

St. Helena

Malta

AFRICA

*Napoleon's conquests*

PRUSSIA
• Berlin
Dresden
•

• Austerlitz

• Vienna

AUSTRIA-
HUNGARY

• Moscow

• Smolensk

RUSSIA

Constantinople
•

BLACK SEA

TURKEY

MEDITERRANEAN   SEA

SYRIA
Acre
•

Abukir  Rosetta

Alexandria•  •  •
Cairo •

EGYPT

*are shown in color*

That day Napoleon had the bitterest experience of his life. Just as Marshal Ney was about to throw his troops against the enemy, twelve hundred men of Ney's corps, turning their arms against the French soldiers, went over to the Coalition. If such treason could happen in his army, then all was lost!

That terrible day also closed on a blood-soaked field, with victory falling to neither side. Napoleon knew, however, that it was a battle lost. He had only to gaze upon the field to know the odds against him. It spread before him as a map which the dead colored with their uniforms like countries on a chart. Italians, Cossacks, and Tartars were there, with Englishmen, Prussians, Saxons, and Hungarians. The whole world was struggling on that field, and he was the man they were seeking to crush.

How could he battle against the whole world? He could hold off the army of the Coalition another day, another week. In the end it would still mean defeat for him. As it was, the battle had cost him sixty-five thousand men. Sadly, he ordered a retreat.

Leaving the generals in charge of the army, Napoleon returned to Paris. He must demand more soldiers from the nation, to fight against the mighty Coalition. Perhaps Marie Louise might have some influence with her father. But Marie Louise had been of no help to him before. She was of no help to him now.

In those dark days he found his only happiness in the King of Rome. Every morning he would carry the child into his study where the toys of the little King were brought. While the boy played with his wooden horse and his soldiers, the Emperor thought of how to save his empire.

It was hard to raise another army. The many years of war had drained the manpower of France. But when the people heard that the Coalition was making ready to invade France, they raised two hundred thousand men for the Emperor. It was not like the earlier armies made up of the finest

ınanhood of France. This was an army of boys and old men.

In January, 1814, the forces of the Coalition actually crossed the border and advanced into France. France, whose victorious armies had conquered a whole continent!

Once again the Emperor prepared to place himself at the head of his army. This time, before he left, he appointed Marie Louise as Regent.

"If the enemy should reach the gates of Paris,"

he said to the National Guard, "I leave in your care what I hold dearest in the world next to France—my wife and child."

Before leaving the palace, early one January dawn, he stole into the room where his little son was sleeping. The nurse started up with a cry of alarm, but the Emperor placed his finger to his lips. By the light of the lamp he gazed on the boy lying so peacefully in his silver cradle. Napoleon remained there for a long time. Then, without a word, he went like a shadow out of the room and into the courtyard.

Mounting his horse, he rode away. The snow had just begun to fall.

For nearly ten weeks he tried to stop the enemy hordes rushing in from every direction. He hurled them back in one battle after another. There was no end to their numbers! Everywhere he was victorious, but not so his generals. Wellington— again that name!—Wellington had beaten another of his marshals! And Marshal Blücher, the old

Prussian war dog, was pushing farther into France. From another quarter Alexander's Cossacks were laying waste the French provinces.

The worst news of all was that the Allies were heading for Paris. In order to lead them off from the city that held his son, Napoleon wrote Marie Louise that he was moving his army toward the Marne, hoping the Allies would follow him there. Blücher, however, captured the courier and Napoleon's plan was laid bare to the enemy.

On the 30th of March, 1814, Paris, undefended, fell to the army of the Coalition.

A week later Napoleon, under pressure from his marshals and everyone else who had any influence over him, agreed to abdicate the throne of France in favor of his son. But the Allies would not consent and forced him to abdicate unconditionally. They had no wish to run the risk of having another Bonaparte repeat Napoleon's history.

So, in a very great hurry, they summoned the royal successor to the French throne. On the

3rd of May, while Napoleon was on his way to exile on the island of Elba, Louis XVIII entered the French capital. As he passed in his carriage, the shopkeepers were busily pulling down Napoleon's emblems of eagles and bees and putting up the Royalist fleur-de-lis.

# [13]

## *News Comes to Vienna*

THE NEWS OF NAPOLEON'S ABDICATION WAS A week old when Wellington received the information at his headquarters at Toulouse, to which his armies had advanced from Spain for the final struggle. That night he and his officers and some of the Royalists of Toulouse celebrated the event at a dinner. Champagne flowed freely and when the toasts were drunk Wellington was the hero of the day.

"Long live the liberator of Spain!"
"Long live the liberator of Portugal!"
"Long live the liberator of France!"

Then someone cried: "Long live the liberator of the world!"

Wellington bowed but took none of it seriously, blaming all that flattery on the fine wines of France. He seldom showed his emotion and he was known to be a man of few words. This time the words were fewer than ever.

"Some coffee," he ordered, hoping it would sober his guests.

His government, however, knew the important part he had played in the downfall of Napoleon, especially during the Peninsular wars, and rewarded Lord Wellington by making him a duke. He was also sent as ambassador to France and then to Spain where, unfortunately, he helped to put on the throne one of the worst despots that Spain ever had, King Ferdinand VII.

Meanwhile at Elba Napoleon was trying to make a new life for himself. His great empire had shrunk to this tiny island from which, on fair days, he could see the outlines of the Corsican mountains. However, he had his faithful Old Guard, veterans of a hundred victories, and he still commanded a small army. The people of the island were proud to have him there and fell in readily with his plans of building new roads, developing the iron mines, increasing the fleet, and enlarging the port. Of course the foreign Commissioners kept their eyes open for any sign that the Eagle might spread his wings and try to fly away.

His many activities did not keep Napoleon from being very unhappy. Marie Louise, who was to

have joined him with their son, preferred to remain in Austria. Like Emperor Francis, she too
had betrayed him. What was his child doing,
Napoleon wondered? Did they ever speak to him
of his father?

It was kinder that Napoleon did not know. The
boy was no longer the King of Rome, no longer
Napoleon; he was now simply "little Bonaparte."
His guns and soldiers and all pictures of his father
had been taken away. Instead of the ribbon of the
Legion of Honor, he had to wear an Austrian order. It was planned to educate him for the Church
so that there would never be any danger of his
seeking the throne of France.

The boy saw the difference in his state. "Where
are my pages?" he asked. "Am I not a king any
more?"

Like Napoleon he was a prisoner, closely
watched so that he would not be influenced by
people who sided with his father. But the boy
loved Napoleon dearly. From the French cham-

berlain whom Marie Louise had taken to Vienna, the child learned all that had happened to Napoleon. He clung to everything that reminded him of his former life, and he could not fall asleep except in the cradle that Marie Louise had carried off to Vienna together with twenty carriage-loads of treasure.

While Napoleon was trying to shorten the long days of exile with many activities, time flew in the Austrian capital, especially after the opening of the Congress of Vienna. Every important European personage was there, Czars and Emperors and Kings, together with ambassadors, ministers, and diplomats. Now that Napoleon had fallen, they were going to decide the fate of Europe.

France had already been taken care of: her boundaries were reduced to those of 1792. Now the Congress of Vienna was going to slice up and distribute Napoleon's conquests among the victors. It was not easy, for the monarchs were greedy. The Czar wanted Poland. The King of Prussia de-

manded Saxony and—why not?—France! England
and Austria didn't like this at all, and made secret
treaties against Russia and Prussia. Often tempers
grew so hot that the former allies came near to being enemies.

For months the Great Powers met over the
Congress tables, making little headway. But they
also had a wonderful time at balls and dinners and
sleigh rides and romps of all sorts. The whole city
was a playground.

It was quite different in Paris. The humiliated
capital had a gloomy time of it under Louis XVIII,
who was a typical Bourbon king, wanting all for
himself and unwilling to give much to the people.
Even those who had welcomed him now thought
sadly of the vanished empire. How was France
going to be treated by the Congress? What more
would be taken from her? How long would France
have to suffer for Napoleon's defeat?

It was 1815 and the Congress was still having a
gay time in Vienna. One night, early in March,

the Empress of Austria was entertaining the distinguished guests at some "living pictures." The curtains of the small stage had just parted on a group of men and women in historical costumes when a courtier hurriedly approached the Empress and whispered something in her ear.

She let out a little shriek. The Court gathered about her. In a few minutes the whole palace was in an uproar. Then the whole city.

Napoleon had escaped from Elba!

# [14]

## *The Hundred Days*

IT WAS TRUE. IN SPITE OF WATCHFUL ENGLISH warships, in spite of the guards, Napoleon had left Elba. It was a very bold stroke. But he had always been a gambler. He now had all to win, or all to lose.

The foreign Commissioners returning to Elba late in February from a little holiday were astonished to find the Emperor's house deserted.

In the harbor the flotilla was gone. The Old Guard, the whole army, the servants had all disappeared. Only Napoleon's mother and his sister Pauline were still there and they claimed to know nothing.

When did Napoleon escape? And how?

It was late afternoon of February 26 when his followers, nearly a thousand men, began quietly embarking on seven frigates. Napoleon had planned his escape a few days earlier and had confided his intention to his most trusted officers. They were all in favor of it, though they did not hide their alarm at such daring. Nevertheless they began making their preparations. They packed nearly a million in gold according to Napoleon's instructions, putting the coins at the bottoms of large packing cases and covering the tops of the cases with books. They stowed away his camp bed, his swords and uniforms and his charts. They issued orders to their men, swearing them to secrecy, and did their business so well that nobody suspected that the ships lying so peacefully in the harbor were really preparing for flight.

Even Napoleon's mother knew nothing of what was happening. Neither did his sister Pauline, who was preparing for a ball and could think of noth-

ing but gowns and jewels. Still, on the evening
of the 25th, both she and her mother noticed
that Napoleon was looking more thoughtful
than usual as they were playing cards together.
Suddenly he left them and walked out into the
garden.

When he did not return his mother followed
him and found him sitting under a tree. At first he
did not speak, but after a while, as she sat down
beside him, he touched her face tenderly and said:
"I'll tell you everything. But you must not breathe
a word of it, not even to Pauline."

Then, in the darkness and the silence, he told
her that he would be leaving the island the following night.

The poor woman shuddered with fear, but she
managed to ask him: "Where will you go?"

"To Paris," he answered. "What do you think
of it?"

At first she was so shocked that she could not
speak. But the old Corsican spirit awoke in her.

"Go, my son," she said. "Go and fulfill your destiny."

Somehow Pauline discovered the secret. With tears in her eyes she gave Napoleon's valet a diamond necklace. "The Emperor will need it if—if he should be unlucky," she sobbed. "Oh, Marchand, if that should happen, promise me you'll never, never leave him!"

Taking advantage of the Commissioners' absence, Napoleon ordered his men to be ready to sail. On the eve of the departure he sent for the governor and the mayor. He told them what he was about to do, thanked them for all their courtesies during his stay at Elba, and added: "I am leaving my mother and my sister in your care, to show you how much I trust you. I am also placing in your charge this country which means so much to me."

After such words the two officials could only express their gratitude for the confidence he placed in them, and they too joined in the plot.

After all his men had embarked Napoleon himself went on board. The little fleet made headway, but in the night the favorable wind died down. Anxiously Napoleon paced the deck. What if the English warships should catch up with him? Then he would be placed beyond hope of escape. Luckily, with the sun, a brisk breeze started up.

Three days later Napoleon landed near Cannes in France.

How would the people greet him? It was Royalist territory through which he would be passing with his thousand men, and he did not want any violence. He therefore avoided the main roads and took the difficult passes across the Alps. Bundled up in his coat of the Chasseurs and with a stick in his hand, he marched side by side with his men.

The villagers recognized him.

"The Emperor!"

The cry echoed from hamlet to hamlet. People rushed out of their houses, hardly believing their ears. The Emperor! But he was a prisoner at Elba!

How did he get away? The daring of the deed excited their admiration. Old men hobbled out of their huts for a glimpse of him. Mothers carried their children in their arms and held them up so that they too could see him and later say: "I saw the Emperor!"

In their enthusiasm the people forgot the years of war and their mourning, and they thought of the glory of France which the armies of occupation had trampled underfoot. They thought of the dreary reign of Louis XVIII, who had brought back the old abuses together with the old monarchy.

The same rejoicing broke out the closer Napoleon got to Paris. Everywhere his old soldiers who had not been allowed to share his exile now joined him, weeping like children. They tore off the King's white cockade which they had been obliged to wear, and pinned on Napoleon's old tricolor, kept carefully in the bottom of their knapsacks for this very day. Generals handed over whole

*The villagers recognized him. "The Emperor!"*

regiments. Marshals, even those who had sworn allegiance to the King, fell into his arms and begged his forgiveness.

"The Eagle will fly from steeple to steeple till it alights on the towers of Notre Dame!" Napoleon promised them.

On, on he marched with an ever-increasing army. Everywhere the roads were lined with frantic crowds. He would have been amused had he seen the rapid changes in the newspaper reports, the nearer he draw to the capital. At first they read: "The Corsican Monster has landed at Cannes!" Then, "The Fiend has reached Grenoble!" Then, "General Bonaparte has stopped off at Lyons!" Later, "Napoleon is at Fontainebleau." Finally, on the 20th of March, "His Majesty the Emperor has entered the palace of the Tuileries."

This amusing account may, or may not, be true. But it is absolute fact that in the march of hundreds of miles from the seacoast to the capital not a shot was fired against Napoleon and not a person was killed. This was perhaps his greatest victory.

But what of Louis XVIII who had had so little time to enjoy his throne? On the night before Napoleon entered Paris the King was helped into his traveling carriage and, in a heavy storm, was driven away to a safe place among friends—till his time would come. For the Bourbons never gave up hope.

Another man had taken quickly to horse the moment he heard of Napoleon's escape—the Duke of Wellington. Gathering troops together on the way, he stood in readiness for whatever might happen.

Paris, in fact all of France, rejoiced at Napoleon's bold gamble to regain power. Privately he was saddened by a bitter disappointment. Marie Louise still refused to come back to him or to let him have his son.

Once the excitement of the heroic march was over, Napoleon settled down to face reality. He knew he would have to go to war. As it was, a more powerful Coalition than the last was forming, vowing to get rid of him at any cost. But France had been bled white by the wars and by the terrible year of occupation. Some of her finest provinces were such wastes that it would take years before anything would grow again. And yet he must prepare!

For the first time in his life the maker of wars would have given anything to avoid war. The Coalition, however, was anxious to make an end of the man who was now an outlaw. This name had been given him, on his escape from Elba, by the representatives of eight nations at the Congress of Vienna.

While he was thus cast out of the family of nations, he was working to give France a democratic Constitution. Indeed, he had a model Constitution drawn up providing freedom of worship, freedom of speech, and all the privileges of democracy.

"I have no wish to engage in any more conflicts," he said to the state body. "Long ago I dreamed of creating a great United States of Europe. Now I shall only work for the peace and unity of France. The ruler will be the first servant of the State."

It was too late. The Allied Powers had declared war.

On a dim June dawn—as how often before!—he prepared to leave the Tuileries to head the army. He did not go to the room where he had taken his last look at the King of Rome more than a year ago. Silently—there was no one to whom to say good-bye—he left the royal palace.

He hoped for victory but when he looked at his army, so young and so old, he wondered. But he still had his forty thousand Old Guards, the heroes of his greatest battles.

Perhaps after a final victory he would never have to go to war again.

# [15]

## *Before Waterloo*

THE DUKE OF WELLINGTON WAS NOT AT ALL pleased with the army at his command. The trained soldiers who had fought under him in Spain had been scattered to all parts of the world where England was having trouble, so he had to make the best of what he could find. With his English, Scottish, and Irish recruits he had Belgians, Dutchmen, Brunswickers, and Hanoverians. He had also the Horse Guards and the cavalry of the Household. This was all well and good, except that there were too many fancy officers and not enough plain fighting men.

"Before you send any more generals," he wrote back to his government, "let me see more troops."

In June, when Napoleon started out, Wellington with his army and old Marshal Blücher, leading the Prussians, were preparing to meet him. Of all generals they were probably the most logical men to take part in the final duel. The Duke of Wellington had for years beaten the French without ever meeting their leader. Blücher had suffered humiliating defeats through Napoleon and had vowed to destroy him. Moreover, they both knew the strength and genius of their enemy.

"The very presence of the man in a battle is equal to so many more thousand fighting men," Wellington said of Napoleon. "I am aware of this, so at least I will not be frightened beforehand."

Meanwhile Napoleon's traveling carriage was dashing along the French roads. The wheat was high in the fields where poppies waved like red banners through the grain. The peasants scarcely turned their heads to see the Emperor fly past.

They had seen that chariot streaking by many a time, and more often than not it meant war.

It was the eve of June 14. Napoleon had left France behind him. Where was the enemy? What numbers would he have to face? He knew that they would be many, many more than his small army. June 14! If only he could meet the enemy on this day, the anniversary of Marengo and Friedland, two of his most glorious victories! He would have another brilliant triumph—and the war would be over.

But there was no engagement. Instead, at daybreak of June 15, he had a staggering moral defeat. One of his generals, with five other officers, deserted and went over to the Prussians. However, Marshal Blücher had the contempt of all decent people for a traitor. When he saw the Royalist cockade which the deserting general had put on to show his change of allegiance, Blücher said: "A scoundrel is always a scoundrel, no matter what kind of badge he pins upon himself."

The fields of Flanders along which Napoleon passed looked like the fields of France, with the same wheat and the same poppies waving. Everything seemed so peaceful in the bright sunlight! Yet soon the ripening grain would be trampled into mud. For while Napoleon was advancing toward Brussels, no less than three hundred thousand men were marching across the plains to meet him.

Wellington, however, was still in the city, quieting the population which had been thrown into a panic at the report that "Boney was coming." Meanwhile Blücher was on his way.

"Who do you think will attack first?" Wellington asked one of his officers. "I or Bonaparte?"

"Bonaparte," the Englishman promptly replied.

The question and answer were full of meaning. Already the two men were seeing again in Napoleon only the Corsican adventurer of long ago—Bonaparte. For that matter, Napoleon had never been anything else to England which had refused to recognize him as he stepped up from rank to rank until he became Emperor of France. The quick answer of the English officer that Bonaparte would be the first to attack, also showed that Napoleon's methods were no longer a secret. The enemy generals had learned them and knew how to prepare for them.

It was the 15th of June. The moment for striking the first blow had come. At one o'clock in the morning Napoleon started out. Two hours later his army, moving in three columns, routed General Ziethen's infantry which tried to keep the French from crossing the Sambre River. Napoleon's Chasseurs broke through easily, sword in hand, and took three hundred prisoners. At the same time, the marines and sappers of the Emperor's Guard went after the enemy to keep them from tearing down the bridges, and to repair those that had been damaged. All through the day the French and the Prussians met in skirmishes, but no real battle was fought until the French captured Charleroi.

Where was Wellington on that first day of battle? Of all places, he was at the house of the Duchess of Richmond, where he and his officers were dancing a very delightful new dance with the ladies. Suddenly a messenger arrived. The Duke of Wellington stopped waltzing and retired to a private room. Napoleon, he learned, was preparing to attack the Prussians in full force. Quietly calling a few trusted officers, so as not to alarm the ladies, Wellington issued his orders.

The music played louder and more gaily. The waltzers kept on waltzing. But as the evening closed the young officers began to disappear one by one, to lead their regiments toward the place of battle.

Wellington studied for a long time the map of Brussels and the surrounding territory.

"Quatre-Bras," he said, pointing to it on the chart. "That is where I shall meet Bonaparte. And if that fails"—here he traced a line north toward Waterloo and cut deep under the name with his thumbnail—"if that fails I shall meet him here."

Early in the morning of the 16th Wellington and his staff rode out to meet Napoleon. For the first time the Duke of Wellington and the Emperor of the French were to engage in combat.

The spirits of the French soldiers had risen after the first victory. As a result, they were eager for

*Wellington was saved by the quickness of his horse*

battle when Marshal Blücher began posting his army on the heights surrounding Ligny, and spreading his cavalry along the plains.

Napoleon went himself to reconnoiter the old Marshal's position.

"We fight Blücher at once," he commanded, "before Wellington and the English have a chance to arrive." Then he turned to Marshal Ney, one of his best commanders. "You go to Quatre-Bras and wipe out Wellington's army when he gets there," he said. "Then fall upon Blücher's flank while I attack his front."

At three o'clock the battle of Ligny began with great fury. The town had strong walls and a deep ravine, the better to protect it. The French advanced with their bayonets, were beaten back, advanced again. Napoleon was everywhere at once. Marshal Blücher, who knew the importance of Ligny in deciding the outcome of the battle which had spread to the surrounding towns, held on stubbornly.

Now losing, now winning, neither side was willing to give up. For five hours the fighting continued without pause. Seven times Ligny was taken by the French and lost again, and still the battle raged with terrible losses to both sides.

At last Napoleon ordered General Erlon to fall on the rear of the enemy. While the horse grenadiers kept up the attack in front, Erlon carried out his maneuvers. The Prussians were scattered, and fled in disorder. Then, as the French grenadiers kept advancing, Blücher was seen to fall from his horse. There was a shout from the French. "Blücher is killed! The day is ours!"

The Marshal, however, though very nearly trampled, was not killed. Ligny fell for the last time. The ravine surrounding its smoking ruins was like a river of blood choked with the bodies of the dead and the dying. Blücher had lost twenty thousand men. The French had lost ten thousand, but had won the battle.

"My star is still with me," said Napoleon, speeding to Quatre-Bras where Ney had not found it so easy to "wipe out" Wellington's army.

Wellington had arrived in the morning to re-enforce the four thousand men of Prince Bernard of Saxe-Weimar. There was no important fighting until the afternoon, when Ney and Wellington engaged in a number of violent tussles. Several times it looked as if the Duke would lose, but his division of Guards arrived and then his brave Scottish Highlanders, and the fighting started up more fiercely than before.

The Duke of Brunswick was killed. At one point Wellington himself was saved only by the quickness of his horse, which leapt to safety with his master clear over a line of Highlanders.

By the time Napoleon arrived at Quatre-Bras, Wellington had retreated to Mont-Saint-Jean and drawn up his army against the hills for the battle he knew would come.

Napoleon took his army to the opposite heights of La Bella Alliance.

# [16]

## *Waterloo*

THE TWO ARMIES WATCHED EACH OTHER FROM
the heights.

Napoleon suggested that his troops attack Wellington at dawn but his generals were against it.
The French were exhausted after Ligny, they
argued, whereas Wellington's men were compara-
tively fresh. The soldiers needed rest. Perhaps
because he was feeling very ill, Napoleon let his
generals have their way.

He then divided his men into two columns,
one of sixty-five thousand which he himself
would command, and one of thirty-six thousand

which he placed under the command of Marshal Grouchy.

"You are to watch and pursue the Prussians," said Napoleon to the marshal. "Pursue them briskly, to keep them from helping the English, and then rejoin the Grand Army as soon as possible. Manage your operations so that you can come to us quickly if we need you."

The morning and afternoon of the 17th passed uneventfully. From time to time Napoleon peered through his glasses at the enemy. Between them spread a field of wheat two miles wide. It was the battlefield of Waterloo.

As he pointed his glass again, impatient that nothing was happening, an officer whom he had sent out to reconnoiter brought back his report. "Wellington has an army of cannon!" the officer cried. "He has mountains of infantry!"

Napoleon thought of his shrunken army and sent for his general staff. For a long time they remained together in his tent, discussing the plans of attack.

In the afternoon the skies turned pitch black and the wind howled. Then the storm broke and the rain came down in torrents, turning the whole field into a lake. It was impossible to place the artillery, impossible to move the troops. Napoleon put on his mask of calm but anyone could see by his fretful pacing up and down that he was very much upset.

In the opposite camp, on the other hand, there was great rejoicing. Each of Wellington's greatest victories had been won after a storm. The English seized upon the weather as a good omen.

Napoleon did not sleep that night. Impatiently he waited for the day to break and the weather to clear so that he could fight the battle he hoped would be his last, the Battle of Waterloo.

It dawned, a peaceful Sunday, the 18th of June. In the little villages the people were getting ready to go to church. The same thing was happening in France and in Austria, too, where his son was a prisoner of Emperor Francis. Napoleon had dreaded this most of all—that his son should fall into the hands of his enemies. But he would rescue him! He would win the coming battle and bring the enemy to terms.

For a long time he gazed at the picture of the King of Rome which he always carried with him. Then he put it down and ordered the bugles to sound and the drums to beat. To the din of the military bands Napoleon's army marched slowly down the slopes in three gleaming columns. Marshal Grouchy went his way.

From Wellington's side the French armored troops looked like gigantic serpents with flashing scales. Fretting with impatience, the red-coated British soldiers waited for the signal.

"If I had had my old Spanish infantry I should have attacked Bonaparte at once," Wellington explained.

Now, however, he gave the signal. "To the last man, to the last moment, fight!"

It was late morning. The ground, soaked through by the heavy rains, was still soggy. In places the infantry plodded ankle-deep in mud. But nothing delayed the battle. At the Emperor's order the French artillery opened the charge upon the English in the middle of the field. At the same time Marshal Ney began his attack from another point with a tremendous force of thirty-two battalions.

As the hours passed, the battle spread from the center throughout the plain of Waterloo. The fields of wheat were trampled to the ground, and the ground itself was pitted and scarred and soaked with blood, two thousand soldiers falling every hour! The quick victory Napoleon had hoped for did not come.

Two o'clock. A German Hussar prisoner, carrying a despatch, was brought before the Emperor who thus learned that a force of thirty thousand

Prussians commanded by General Bülow was on its way to Wellington.

"Bah! They exaggerate!" said Napoleon, throwing the despatch aside. "Besides, if that is so, Grouchy is probably after them."

Nevertheless he ordered a charge of the cavalry to meet the Prussians and commanded two of his generals to stand ready to crush Bülow with all the means in their power.

Wellington's forces, meanwhile, were holding firm though he lost hundreds of soldiers with every minute of fighting. La Haye Sainte, a cluster of buildings taken by the French, was disputed by Picton and his British brigades. The smoke of musketry fire hid the contestants from view. But even through the noise of battle Picton's voice was heard, roaring "Charge!"

As the smoke cleared the French were seen to scatter and La Haye Sainte fell to the English. They took three thousand French prisoners and two Eagles, Napoleon's standards. But among the

English dead Wellington found the brave Picton. Wellington had scarcely reported the victory when La Haye Sainte was recaptured.

In such deadly give-and-take the hours passed.

Wellington's troops were now terribly thinned by the charges and countercharges. But knowing that Bülow was on his way, he encouraged his soldiers. Still, he was heard to mutter: "Would to God night or Bülow would come!"

Napoleon, pointing his glass toward the darkening distance, also made a wish. "Oh, that Grouchy were here!"

Suddenly, as if his wish had been granted, he saw a faint cloud of blue on the horizon. Grouchy with the reënforcements! The next moment Napoleon's heart sank as he remembered that the Prussians, too, wore blue uniforms! Hoping against hope, he threw his remaining forces into battle—all except his beloved Guard, his heroes, the last remaining companions of his glory.

The cloud of blue advanced. The English set up a shout. It was Bülow!

"Why does Grouchy not come?" Napoleon repeated in despair.

The Marshal, misunderstanding an order he had received during the battle, was waiting, within hearing of the cannon of Waterloo, for Napoleon's command to march.

The sun was slowly sinking but the battle only gained in fury. Wellington rushed his men to the brigade of English Guards, knowing that they would be receiving the full force of Napoleon's attack.

At this moment the rattle of musketry echoed in the distance. "Ah! There's Grouchy at last!" exclaimed the Emperor.

Without waiting to find out if it were true, one of his generals flew to announce the good news to the army. "Marshal Grouchy is on his way! The Guard is going to charge! Take heart! It will soon be all over with the English!"

The weary last remnant of Napoleon's army started up with new courage and energy. "Long live the Emperor!" they cried. "Forward! Forward!"

Napoleon, in desperate hope, threw into battle his Young Guard and his Middle Guard. He still held back the Old Guard, the bravest of the brave, the terrifying warriors with their fierce mustaches and waving plumes—the unconquered, the unconquerable.

The columns were mowed down like grass by Wellington's artillery and the cavalry brigade. Still, still the French waited for Grouchy. But it was General Ziethen whose fire they had heard— and he brought thirty thousand to help the English!

The Young and the Middle Guard began to retreat in frantic disorder.

"Stand up!" Wellington called to his cavalry. "Now! Now is your chance!"

The English gave the retreating grenadiers volley after volley.

Napoleon had no choice. He must call on his last reserves. With a breaking voice he addressed his Old Guard.

"Heroes of my triumphs! The fate of the Empire is in your hands!"

"Long live the Emperor!" they answered him.

Like an onrushing wave they moved toward the center of the English lines.

Wellington, heading the cavalry, now took off

his hat and, waving it in the direction of the Old Guard, again gave the command: "Charge!"

In the fire of cannon and musketry the Old Guard advanced toward the mighty enemy, across a field heaped with mountains of dead. They fought like demons, they fought like angels, but they were not immortal, and they fell.

The English, appalled by such heroism, called to them to surrender.

"The Old Guard dies! It does not surrender!"

They died.

With them died Napoleon's glory.

# [17]

## *The Carriage at Bullock's*

IT WAS LATE JANUARY, 1816 AND PICCADILLY IN
the heart of London was as busy as a beehive. The
owner of Bullock's Museum looked out on the
crowd and rubbed his hands. He knew that nine
out of ten carriages would stop in front of his door
to let out fine ladies and gentlemen. He knew that
ninety-nine out of every hundred persons who had
no carriages would be walking into his museum.

He had advertised his newest exhibit all over the
city. But he could have saved himself the trouble
for nearly everybody in the world had heard about
it. Thousands of people in Italy, Spain, Austria,

Poland and Russia had even seen it. But not until recently had it come to England.

It was the military carriage of Napoleon Bonaparte. He had left it behind after the Battle of Waterloo. Wellington had sent it as a gift to the Prince Regent who had sold it to Bullock's.

The older people had solemn faces when they looked at the blue-green carriage with crimson wheels. Many visitors were dressed in black because they had lost sons and husbands at Waterloo. The children, on the other hand, ran around the carriage joyfully. All their lives the shadow of Napoleon had hung over England. There wasn't a boy or girl there who had not trembled at the words: "Boncy will get you if you don't watch out!"

Some of the children carried a little book. Piles of it were for sale on a table, and they went very briskly. It was called *The Coach that Nap ran from: an Epic Poem* and it had been brought out especially for the exhibit by the Juvenile Library of the London Museum.

"Look!" the children would cry out to each other excitedly as they clustered about the carriage. "It is just the way the book says."

An attendant asked one of the boys to read the description aloud and, after a little coaxing, the lad obliged in a singsong voice:

> *The wonderful coach from which Nappy flew,*
> *At Bullock's Museum is open to view.*
> *And if you will please to take a walk in,*
> *The whole will be shown as neat as a pin.*
> *His watch, knives and forks, and cup you will see,*
> *Besides his gold pot, for making his tea.*
> *His plates, spoons and bedstead and, to be short,*
> *His silver utensils of every sort:*
> *And, if you wish, you may have a step through*
> *The carriage so famous from fam'd Waterloo.*

As the boy read, the guard pointed to the things mentioned in the book. The young audience and some of their elders exclaimed with surprise at the richness of even the most common utensil.

In a little while a dignified gentleman with a beard like that of the King of Spades walked up to the carriage and told how Napoleon had left it behind after his terrible defeat. He pointed out other articles in it, a brandy case, a wash basin, a dressing case—all decorated with a crown and engraved with a big N. Each of the articles was made of solid gold.

"When the carriage was taken there were a great number of diamonds and other precious things," he said, "but these I am not able to show you."

Everybody sighed with disappointment. However, they were soon interested again when the man showed them the bullet-proof panels of the coach, the holsters on the doors, and a double-barreled pistol lying on the seat where Napoleon had left it.

"Imagine how desperate he must have been

when he fled," the dignified gentleman remarked. "Not because he left his gold and diamonds, but because he did not even take a weapon to defend himself. He was too desperate to want to live."

"'Pon my honor, the fellow is right," said a soldier who was standing near by.

Among the other exhibits were uniforms, swords, and muskets, together with several of Napoleon's standards and maps. There were also pictures of the Duke of Wellington and of Napoleon. Those of Wellington were surrounded by the crown of victory.

Indeed, after Waterloo the Duke had become a national hero. The Prince Regent himself wrote him a letter in which he said: "Even the genius of the Corsican could not withstand the supreme genius of our own hero."

Never before had a military man enjoyed the rewards and honors that were heaped upon Wellington. He had so many titles that it took several minutes merely to say them over. He lived a long

and distinguished life. When he was buried in 1852, twenty thousand mourners followed his body to St. Paul's.

Meanwhile, what of Napoleon?

During that final tragic hour of battle he joined the last of his Old Guard and sought death in the field. But they, who had never feared for their lives, feared for his. "Go! Go!" one of them commanded with gruff affection. "Can't you see death does not want you?" Then some officers seized the Emperor's bridle and dragged him away.

Death did not want him because Napoleon had still to work out his destiny.

Once more he abdicated, trying in vain to save some shred of his empire for the son whom he was never to see again as long as he lived.

Louis XVIII again filled the French throne. All the kings whom Napoleon had made were now no more important than the figures in a deck of cards. His family went into exile. Joseph, once King of Naples and King of Spain, managed to escape to the United States, taking with him a fortune in millions. Josephine had died. Marie Louise never returned to her husband.

Three weeks after Waterloo Napoleon was a hunted man. But he still had faithful followers, willing to share his fate. They advised him to escape to America. But it was impossible. English vessels were watching the seacoast everywhere.

At last he threw himself upon the mercy of the Prince Regent of England.

"I have reached the end of my political career," he wrote to the Prince, "and come to sit down by the hearths of the English people. I place myself under the protection of their laws, which I claim from Your Royal Highness as the most powerful and the most generous of my enemies."

He never sat down by the hearths of the English people. It would have been too dangerous for the peace of the world. The Duke of Wellington now remembered the island of St. Helena, that lonely bit of volcanic rock in the middle of the South Atlantic Ocean.

There, with his devoted friends, Napoleon spent the last six years of his life.

"When I die," he used to say, "the world will heave a great sigh of relief."

It did.

Napoleon, however, left behind him a legend and a moral lesson. He showed what a man can accomplish through strength of purpose, courage, and imagination. He destroyed the last remnants of feudalism in Europe and abolished the Inquisition in Spain. He helped to build the modern code of laws. He encouraged art and science and education.

But once he gained power he paired it with his colossal ambition. The two, like fiery steeds driven recklessly for his own glory, plunged him and his empire to destruction. So great was his fall at Waterloo that since then all defeat has been known by its name.

# INDEX

# INDEX